Between Black and White

Msg York L. Parm Sr.
65 E Main St
Ayer, MA 01432

Between Black and White

From Evanston
to Englewood
to Everywhere

Dr. Tony Bethel

Copyright © 2015 by Dr. Tony Bethel.

Library of Congress Control Number: 2015904629
ISBN: Hardcover   978-1-5035-5677-5
               Softcover   978-1-5035-5678-2
               eBook   978-1-5035-5679-9

Print information available on the last page.

Rev. date: 05/19/2015

To order additional copies of this book, contact:
Xlibris
1-888-795-4274
www.Xlibris.com
Orders@Xlibris.com
696292

To H.S., let the conversation begin.

In all thy ways acknowledge him, and he shall direct thy paths.
—Proverbs 3:6

To Landon Xavier Scanlon
May you always be comfortable in that space between black and white.

To my ancestors both black and white that made me write this book.

To my Lady "A"
My sugar, my spice, my salty and nice.

For what is a man profited, if he shall gain
The whole world, and lose his own soul?
—Matthew 16:26

Chapter One

I have wondered for a number of years now why my great-great-great-grandmother would have a Hindi name if she was from West Africa. To the best of my knowledge, Nidra was her birth name. This differs so much from my distant cousin Alex Haley's experience where his ancestor had a traceable African name, as well as certain words this ancestor (Kunta Kinte) used to identify the area of Africa that he was from and everyday things/objects he dealt with. Knowing that reminds me of the importance of our language/culture, two things that the slaves of the African diaspora were denied of. This lack of self-knowledge and the resultant resentment makes identification/assimilation into the dominant culture difficult at best. If someone is not willing to embrace/acknowledge your culture, how can they be angry when you don't embrace their culture/language? There are many "mixtures" of African Americans, so how should we identify ourselves? Why bother looking back anyway? I would say in order to know your direction, you have to know where you have been.

I have European American friends who were adopted or are foster children, and they grew up in well-to-do households with excellent parents. Yet they still have this yearning to know exactly where they were from—their ancestry and their genetic makeup. It is our nature as human beings to know about ourselves, which is difficult since there is so little documentation in slave families (unless they were genetically related to the slave holders or had a key position where they were enslaved). In my family fortunately/unfortunately, I was able (with the assistance of my uncle, Dr. Wilbert Jackson) to trace back to my great-great-great-grandmother Nidra (on my father's side). I have always wondered about this tall, slender, strong, dignified woman of West Africa and how she was brought here as a little girl. She was too small for chains but tied up below decks on a slave ship. If that little girl had not survived that trip, I would not be here writing these words about her—how ironic. I also read in my family documents that she/Nidra worked in the fields and could "work as hard as any man" and often "whistled while she worked."

The name Nidra is Hindi. Nidra was the goddess of sleep (I am pretty sure my Nidra got little of that, being a slave). To the best of my knowledge, I do not have any Indian blood (maybe some native/indigenous people). I have always been intrigued by her name and its real meaning. My guess is my great-great-great grandmother Nidra used sleep as a defense mechanism for all the madness that was going on around her—if that were at all possible. Being a little girl, it's a shame to think of what her eyes have seen.

It is estimated she was born in the late 1700s and arrived prior to 1810. As a worker in the fields and blossoming into a young lady, she drew attention. Unfortunately, it happened to be the slave owner who was paying attention. Going past the details, needless to say she became pregnant with my great-great grandmother, Caroline. After Caroline's birth, I do not have any more information on Nidra, although I can trace Caroline's father (William Bethell Jr.) all the way back to the late 1500s in York, England to a Richard Bethell. What a stark contrast in identity. I could tell you all my European components (English, Scotch Irish, German, Dutch, Swedish), yet I could not tell you with certainty any of the African tribes in my family, which is a shame. It is also a testament to the suppression of knowing about one's (African) past and the enforcement of white culture (in more ways than one).

Caroline must have been very fair and very beautiful. She was not for the fields, although the fields would have been a better fate than she was subjected to. She was used for breeding purposes, not only with other slaves but also with the slave owner's son (her own half-brother), Samuel. They would have three children together (Ollie Minta, Oscar, and my great grandfather, Charles Henry). Caroline had knowledge of herbs/plants and healing that her mother Nidra had taught her. This elevated Caroline's status (somewhat) within the Bethell household. In fact, when there was a local smallpox epidemic, she went to one of the local plantations to nurse the sick. There is a saying, "No good deed goes unpunished," but you see, upon her return from the neighboring plantation, Caroline was pregnant. What is even stranger about the story is that the neighboring family was also quite wealthy, powerful, and fancied slave women (who would believe them or take up their cause). The story that was crafted about Caroline's pregnancy was that she got pregnant by a native/indigenous person, Hillum, who lived at that plantation. I am skeptical about this because the child that was born, Ella Belle, who had long dark hair that was very straight, also had an "encounter" with one of the men of this neighboring plantation to produce a child named Jenny Lind Bethel. Jenny Lind Bethel was named by my great-uncle Oscar for Jenny Lind, the "Swedish Nightingale" that toured the country around that time.

Many years later, Jenny Lind Bethel and her husband Mr. J. Holt would be one of the twenty-nine families of the wagon train that would go from Alamance County, North Carolina, to Lauderdale County in Tennessee, which also included Chicken George, Tom Murray, his wife Irene, and their daughter Cynthia, who was cousins/sisters with Jenny Lind Bethel (depending on which story you believe).

Caroline's children with Samuel Bethell (Ollie Minta, Oscar, and Charles Henry) had a different status—they were slaves, but also family. The saving grace for the boys, but not so much for their sister, was that their appearance and their other features appeared white. My great-grandfather's appearance was described as "Nordic", and my great-uncle Oscar's features, as well as his behavior, was totally white.

My great-aunt Ollie Minta did not fare as well as her brothers. She was fair and extremely beautiful, but technically, she was not white, so she was victimized by some of the men of the household/family. Starting at the age of thirteen, she was seduced by an adult cousin to the Bethells by the name of James McCadden. He gave her his name on a piece of paper, saying this is the name of the child. She would also have another child by another cousin, and the child's name would be George Williamson.

When someone told Oscar he was a slave (at the age of sixteen), he cried the whole day. This was the same young man who talked his white half-brother out of a horse so that he could have one of his own. These children were taught alongside the other white children in the household. My great-grandfather Charles Henry was said to have been quite a good student. Oscar was clever and a deal maker. Ollie Minta, being much older, took care of the children of the household (as well as her own). What a bum deal to be both slave and female. (Beauty was a curse.) When I think of all this, I wonder, are we what we are by genetics, socialization, or both? What really is African American?

I have heard people (both black and white) argue about President Obama's ancestry and being the first African American president since his mother was white. I would counter by saying that in the truest sense, President Obama is African American—that is, his father was African and his mother was American.

My great-grandfather was born in 1854, but his mother Caroline would continue to have children until 1860. After the war, Samuel and Caroline would marry and move away.

Also after the war, Chicken George came back to Alamance County, North Carolina, after visiting the new frontier of West Tennessee near Henning in Lauderdale County. When he came back, he excitedly told his family about West Tennessee and that the whites there desperately needed people there to help build the community. People like blacksmiths, carpenters, brick masons, farmers, cooks, tailors/seamstresses. Think of all the things these people did as slaves; now they could go to Tennessee and get paid and/or barter for their goods and services. All they needed to do now was get there and clear the land.

As you can guess, word got out to the other local plantations, which also included the Bethels and the Holts. This is significant because Rev. Jerry Holt married Ollie Minta Bethel, and Ollie Minta asked if she could take her two boys as well as her brother Charles Henry Bethel (my great-grandfather) with them. Reverend Holt agreed. My cousin Jenny Lind Bethel also came. This is significant because she and Cynthia Murray (Alex Haley's grandmother) were sisters/cousins, depending on the family story you chose to believe.

There were twenty-eight wagons initially, but an additional twenty-ninth was made for the white overseer who asked to come (he and his wife). Since he had worked closely with the slaves rather than being an overseer, he was allowed to come, which again makes me wonder about identity and who (and why) we chose to be in certain groups. Theirs would be the only white family on the journey, and ironically he was also named George. At the front of the wagon train, you had Chicken George, his son Tom, Tom's wife Irene, and their family, which included Cynthia, and the last wagon had George, the white, former overseer, and his wife. Various families dropped off along the way, the majority settling in Lauderdale County in West Tennessee, not too far from the Mississippi River.

Charles Henry Bethel, James McCadden, and George Rufus Williamson would later go south to neighboring Tipton County and the city of Covington. Since these young men were builders, they found much work in the bustling Covington. Charles Henry Bethel's brick masonry may still be seen today in the form of houses, churches (Canaan Baptist Church is on the National Registry of Historic Places), and the courthouse in Covington's town square (featured in the movie *A Family Thing* with James Earl Jones and Robert Duvall, which was released in the mid-1990s). He built buildings for both black and white and had great respect in both communities. He was held in high regard for his skill and creativity. He was also a firm believer in faith and education. How fitting he would have the last name Bethel because in Hebrew, it means "house of God". There is (I believe) a Welsh meaning, which comes out to be the "son of Ithell." Given my DNA results, my origins are more English than Jewish. In fact, most of my white family members were/are English, Scotch Irish, German, Dutch, and Swedish.

It is such a sad situation that I could tell you all about the European side of my family, and I could not tell you a single African tribe (that I know for sure) that I am related to. What a shame. I am embarrassed.

Going back to the courthouse, my cousins Michael and John Edwards's father, Mack Edwards, is in the movie playing dominoes in front of the courthouse (he is the one in the straw hat) at the very beginning of the movie. The reason I mention the movie *A Family Thing* is not only is it a good movie, but it also touches upon identity and self-acceptance, some of the things I am writing about now (how eerie). For further eeriness, just look at the bust of Nathan Bedford Forrest (originator of the Ku Klux Klan) on the front lawn of the courthouse. The Klan originated in East Tennessee, in a place called Pulaski (of all names).

My great-grandfather Charles Henry Bethel was married three times (It's not what you think). The first two wives died before he married my great-grandmother Callie Hurt, who was a school teacher at the time. Callie Hurt was from Jackson, Tennessee, and was considerably younger than Charles Henry. In fact, Charles Henry was closer to Callie's father in age. Albert Hurt (who was half German) lived with Callie and Charles later. I heard it was not uncommon for successful older men to marry much younger ladies at this time (I think that goes throughout all time).

Callie and Charles Henry Bethel had eight children together (see diagram below): Theodore Herman, who my father, brother, and nephew are named after; Juanita; Charlyne; Samuel, who my grandfather and elder brother are named after; Thomas; Beverly; Hertha; and Mentha, named after Ollie Minta, Charles Henry's sister.

Theodore Herman Bethel was the eldest of the third set of children. He was a very educated man, and he got his bachelor's degree from Lane College in Jackson, Tennessee, one of the historically black colleges in the area. He became an educator and quite a gifted musician.

Charles H. Bethel –– Callie Hurt Bethel

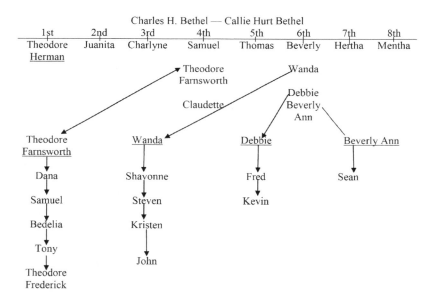

Charles H. Bethel — Callie Hurt Bethel

1st	2nd	3rd	4th	5th	6th	7th	8th
Theodore Herman	Juanita	Charlyne	Samuel	Thomas	Beverly	Hertha	Mentha

The second child was Juanita. She was very creative and artistic. She died of Influenza in the early 1920s.

The third child Charlyne who was very close to her elder sister would die one year after her.

The fourth child was my grandfather, Samuel Farnsworth. He was the entrepreneur and free spirit of the family. He learned brick masonry, but he would also own a few of the buildings on the black side of town.

My grandfather was named Samuel after Charles Henry's father, who was white. My grandfather was a very popular man, and in his early adulthood, he met Cordelia Hall. Soon after their romance, Cordelia became pregnant with my father, and Samuel and Cordelia married. My father was Theodore Farnsworth Bethel. The Theodore name came from my great-uncle—the educator, and musician, who was my grandfather's elder brother and the first to graduate from college. Not bad, considering his father Charles Henry was born into slavery. We will come back to my father and his lineage, but I would like to talk about the remaining four siblings (my great-aunts and uncles) who were great in their own right.

The fifth child was Thomas Curtis, who would become an educator and brick mason. He was also a WWII veteran. He got his bachelor's degree from Lane College and pledged Kappa Alpha Psi. In later years, the Memphis chapter of Kappa Alpha Psi would award my uncle with the title "man of the year," which is a very prestigious award. There was also a newspaper article on my uncle's life as well as his wife Jewel (Strong) Bethel, who was also an educator and member of Alpha Kappa Alpha Sorority. My uncle served in the Tipton County school district for nineteen years, and retired from that job. He was revered as a vocational education teacher. Many of his students, both black and white, would win awards for various skills involved in the building trades, from brick masonry to general electrical work and plumbing. Many of his students would go on to become successful contractors in their own right. My uncle died at eighty-four, having lived a full and successful life.

The sixth child was Beverly Vernon Bethel. He and my grandfather Samuel were the only two out of the eight children that would have children of their own. Uncle Beverly was very unique in that he took up carpentry, which was totally different from his father and brothers, yet he was a gifted carpenter as well as educator. He would come to the North to finish high school at Englewood High School in Chicago. And would go on to become an educator, coach, carpenter, and contractor in the Chicago area. He had three children with Lurline (Prestwood) Bethel, who was also in education and a gifted seamstress. Their three daughters (my cousins) are Wanda, Deborah, and Beverly Ann. My cousin Wanda is a successful administrator in the healthcare system just south of Chicago. My cousin Deborah was a very successful principal in the Chicago Public School System. When she retired, she had thirty-four years in. And their youngest sister, Beverly Ann, is working in healthcare. We are a year apart, and we both grew up in Englewood. We would spend a lot of time together growing up in Englewood.

The seventh child was my aunt Hertha, who was very reserved yet accomplished in her own right. She did not go to war, but she spent more than twenty years in a federal service job at Fort Sheridan, Illinois, working for the United States Army. Although she did not have any children of her own, she was definitely a mother figure to her young nieces and nephews (myself included). She loved to watch horse racing and went to various tracks in the Chicago land area. She would always make me this great clam dip for my birthday; and later, when I would have children of my own she would make these elaborate Jell-O molds with fruit that my young children would call "jelly mold." She would retire and move to Covington with her younger sister Mentha and Mentha's husband, Dr. Wilbert Jackson. They lived in an elaborate ranch-style home on none other than Bethel Street, named after their father, my great-grandfather, Charles Henry Bethel, who had contributed so much to Covington, Tennessee.

Last but certainly not least was Aunt Mentha—number eight. She was named after Charles Henry's elder sister, Ollie Minta. Aunt Mentha was very outspoken. She was a woman who did not mince her words or suffer fools. She could be sweet and charming but anyone who would let their guard down or not give her credit for being the talented capable woman that she was - watch out. She, like Aunt Hertha, had no children of her own, yet she (also like Aunt Hertha) left an indelible mark on us children. She told us to stand straight, to use proper English, to utilize all your talents, to not be anyone's fool, and to get the best education possible. She worked for Sivart Realty (one of the few African American-owned real estate agencies in Chicago). So, although she did not build buildings, she dealt them out like a master dealer.

She would be married four times. Her third and fourth husbands, I knew about. The third was Lloyd Washington, a successful printer, who, along with his brother, had a prosperous family business until his death. The fourth husband was Dr. Wilbert Jackson, who was a psychology professor at Chicago Teacher's College before he came to Chicago State University. He would later retire from Chicago State, and he and my aunt would move South to live in a sprawling ranch-style home with my Aunt Hertha on Bethel Street.

Uncle Wilbert was never idle, and he treated me like a son and was a major influence in me getting my BS in psychology from the University of Illinois at Urbana-Champaign. Uncle Wilbert was an excellent researcher. Being inspired by Alex Haley's book *Roots* and our family stories, he decided to do research on the Bethel family. It is from his data/research that I am able to write this book. Uncle Wilbert also taught psychology part time at a junior college in Dyersburg, Tennessee. He was an avid tennis player, and after his untimely death from a stroke, a tennis invitational championship was started bearing his name in Covington, Tennessee. He and my aunt Mentha were in fact featured in *Ebony* magazine (November 1991) in an article which dealt with active seniors.

After my aunts and uncles died, my cousin Wanda was responsible for a lot of the upkeep and maintenance of the family properties in Covington. She is the eldest of the surviving Bethel children of Beverly and Samuel's offspring. She is followed by her sister Debbie, then my sister Dana, then my brother Samuel, then my sister Bedelia (Dee), then my cousin Beverly Ann, then me. And last, but certainly not least, was my little brother Theodore Frederick who died in 2002, ten years my junior. I have a nephew by my little brother Theodore, Teddy Jr., who was born in 1998. My nephew is a multi-sport B student who has his eyes on the prize of college. My brother would be so pleased.

Now we return to my grandfather, Samuel Farnsworth Bethel. He was the favorite of Charles Henry Bethel, just as my uncle Beverly was the favorite of Mama Callie. I grew up listening to stories of the bravado of my daring grandfather, from his childhood throughout adulthood. I remember a story where my grandfather had a chemistry set and he would make certain compounds/concoctions and have them explode. I remember another story of him wanting a slice of cake Mama Callie made for the church ladies and she specifically forbade him to have any. Being the ingenious and crafty person that he was, he would cut underneath the cake to make it hollow, and so from the outside, it looked great. However, when the ladies cut into the cake, what a surprise they received! I can't remember what his punishment was; since Mama Callie was a school teacher, I am sure it was significant and tough.

There were also acts of kindness and bravery, like when Mama Callie would punish his little sister Hertha by putting her in the closet. Aunt Hertha, being afraid of the dark, was quite upset. My grandpa found/made a back entrance to the closet, and he would sneak in and sit with her through her punishment. There was also a time when, for some reason, two white boys tried to beat up my grandpa. Mama Callie, wielding a broom, beat the boys until they let go. This was unheard of at this time in the South. Since the Bethels (with the exception of my grandpa) were rather fair and their features similar to white, as well as their status/history within the community (they helped build Covington, Tennessee), many times the whites turned a blind eye to their behavior. How else could you explain a Bethel Street in Covington, Tennessee, if that black man did not make a significant contribution to the town as a whole?

I believe the cemeteries are segregated. I also believe that there is still a Confederate soldiers' graveyard which is still preserved. I also remember a story about my uncle Beverly. He got into a fight with the son of a prominent white man in the community and beat him. The white man came by the Bethel house wanting to see my uncle. When he saw that Uncle Beverly was smaller than his boy, the man left, embarrassed.

All was not peaches and cream, especially in the South. I guess it was the day-to-day indignities and lack of opportunity that gave my relatives incentive to go north to Chicago. Mama Callie had a sister, Aunt Alberta (named after my great-great-grandfather Albert since he had no sons), who lived up in Chicago but had no biological children of her own. One by one my relatives went, from my grandfather to my uncles Thomas and Beverly, and my aunts Hertha and Mentha would stay until their retirement in the 1980s. My uncle Beverly stayed until his death in 1982 (a few months before my father).

The year 1982 would be a tough year for the Bethels: Mama Callie died that winter at the age of 104 after a long and productive life, my uncle Beverly died that summer, and my father would die that fall—a Bethel almost each season that year.

That was the beginning of my senior year at the University of Illinois at Urbana-Champaign. I had wanted to become a doctor at the time, but after my father died, I lost my ambition for a while. I did graduate on time in 1983 with a BS in psychology. I took a management trainee position upon graduation, but I felt unmotivated. I believed my mom wanted me to live up to the person that my father was. But I was a totally different person with different values, and I wanted nothing more than to leave the rural area. The opportunity came through the U.S. Navy. I took the ASVAB (the military's SAT), and my score was in the 90s. Everything was open, including the position of officer, but for some strange reason (maybe pride), I let my recruiter talk me into nuclear power training (big mistake) I was not cut out for this program. I lasted a few months, but I would receive an academic drop from the program.

Because of my military bearing, and also because of my past record, which included being the "Honor Man" of my boot camp company 272 at Great Lakes, Illinois, I was still thought to have potential. I was offered a chance at submarine school, which was/is an all volunteer force. Submarine school was in Groten (rhymes with "rotten"), Connecticut. Ironically, there wasn't anything rotten in Groten, and I wanted to learn about subs. I made new friends, and I did well enough to earn a spot on the prized (at this time) fleet ballistic missile submarines. They had more room, so they could carry (potentially) sixteen nuclear missiles. I was on submarines from 1985 until I obtained a commission to go to Officer Candidate School in Newport, Rhode Island.

It was also in the late 1980s that the first Bethel-Holt-Holcomb-Lea family reunion was held in Henning, Tennessee, in Lauderdale County. Cousin Alex Haley showed up. I could not be present because of my military obligations, but my uncle Wilbert gleaned a lot of information and, in turn, would do his own research on the Bethel family. He sent off for numerous records in Chicago, Illinois; Covington, Tennessee; as well as the starting point, Alamance County, North Carolina, near Burlington. His research was groundbreaking for our family.

Still, no one knows about Nidra's tribe or her origins or her name's true meaning. The mystery continues.

Chapter Two

I was the love child of Theodore F. Bethel and Ida Wooley. He was twenty-seven and she was nineteen. He was married, and she worked for him at a restaurant that he had with his wife Alice (my older sibling's mom). My father had a family before I came along. There was Dana who was six at my birth, there was Sam that was four at my birth, and there was my sister Bedelia (Dee) who was almost two at my birth. To the best of my knowledge, we always had a great relationship and viewed each other as siblings and not half-brothers/sisters. How do you cut someone in half anyway? Our relationship is a testimony to *all* our parents that we should know one another.

Needless to say, the affair and the result of it (me—among other things—would lead to a divorce from a great lady, Alice J. Broadway. I was around seven when my parents would marry. I don't know why I have felt such guilt over the years over this situation, yet I am eternally grateful to my mom Ida M. Wooley for having me and not aborting me, giving me up for adoption, or having me be raised by someone else.

I have always admired and looked up to my siblings, and we would spend the summers with one another. Starting I believe when I was six or seven, we would go down to Covington, Tennessee via car. I remember my first trip with my siblings down south (they had gone a few times before me). I was so excited. I was with my big brother and sisters—I felt so cool.

This would be my first time meeting my relatives down south. Mama Pearl was my great-grandmother (my father's mom's mom), who lived by herself on Bledsoe Street. I would also spend some time with my Aunt Katie (Mama Pearl's other daughter). My grandma (Cordelia) had died years ago—I never knew her, except through photos. It was fun to have two different residences during the summer, to see different relatives, and to play with different kids on both sides of town.

Aunt Katie (my grandma's sister) was a school teacher and a kind and loving woman. She was an excellent cook as well as a beautiful person. She and Mama Pearl made sure we attended church every Sunday. We called Aunt Katie "Army" because when our father was small, he could not say Auntie, so "Army" was the word he (and we) would use.

We spent our summers playing with the neighborhood kids and our cousins, enjoying our summers, enjoying nature. Although we were not rich, I did feel privileged by having all this love around me. When my siblings and I would go "up town" on Saturdays, it was quite a treat. We would always make sure we visited the Benjamin Franklin's store. There we would look at the toys and sometimes buy a few, as well as get some candy and some slushies to drink on those hot summer days. It was so ironic that the stores surrounded the courthouse, as if the courthouse was the center and everything else revolved around it. It would be many years later before I would realize our great-grandfather did the brick work of/built this courthouse.

The city seemed segregated by choice rather than by design. There were exceptions. I remember one of those businesses being my Uncle Lonnie's barbeque pit that he owned with his brother Giles. They would own this establishment for over forty years. In business, they say "location, location, location." In this case it was very true, since this business was established during segregation, and it was on a major bus route going from south to north and vice-versa. This was one of the few places an African American could get a hot meal and not be harassed which was also owned by African Americans. The irony of this business was that whites heard about how great the barbeque sandwiches were here and they too started coming. So picture this: black and white under the same roof, but people chose to sit at different tables. The place was too small for a "white" or "colored" section, so everyone just ate as close to their group as possible.

I don't remember playing with any white children down south at any time, although in Evanston, Illinois, at my grammar school, the majority of my class and school were white, and I had many friends that were "different." I remember a story told by my dad about a group of kids playing tag. Somehow a little white girl got in the game (this was the mid

1940s). My father was "it," so he ran to tag the white girl. Mama Pearl happened to see from the porch and screamed for him to stop. This was a strange time in America—the "dark ages" (pun intended).

I remember another story from my father when during the depression, a white salesman was walking up the walk and said, "Hey, Anty." Before he could step foot on the porch, she said, "Now wait a minute. I don't remember having any white nephews." That got him straight, and his tone changed.

Papa Jim, Mama Pearl's husband, may have been a little crippled by polio, but he was custodian of the local school and a Mason (the organization). I remember many Sundays spent in Collins AME Church (AME means African Methodist Episcopal). Mama Pearl played piano in church and taught piano when she was younger. My Aunt Katie "Army" sang when she was younger. I still remember one of my favorite hymns, "Blessed Assurance," playing in the background. I believe I started going down south with my siblings when I was six in the summer of 1968, a few months after Dr Martin Luther King's assassination and before Bobby Kennedy's assassination—maybe.

I was aware of color differences from a very early age because I attended kindergarten, first, and second grade at Noyes Elementary School in Evanston, Illinois, not too far from Northwestern University. Noyes is now a center for the performing arts as well as an art gallery. Most of my early experiences with whites were positive. I do remember my occasional fights with white students. A few were based on color, but I would say more were based on just being kids. My classmates were American, German, English, Swiss, Eastern European, Hispanic/Latino, and African/Carribean, so from a very early age I learned how to deal with many different types of people. I remember after Dr. King was assassinated, some of the upper grades (fifth and up) put on a play about his life and accomplishments. I don't remember a lot, but from a person who never experienced forced segregation, the play definitely made us understand why Dr. Martin Luther King was important to all of us in ways a child could understand. It made me sad that he was gone.

My mom took great chances and made great sacrifices for my education. I remember the times when it was just us two very fondly. She and my dad stressed the importance of education. Looking back now I get it, since they both were educated in the segregated South.

My parents married when I was around seven. We moved in with my father not too long after that. It was a light green house on West Sixty-Seventh Street, right across from Ogden Park in Englewood (it still stands today but the front of the house is different). Evanston had been a great preparation for me not only in education, but also in dealing with whites.

There was a slight culture shock (at first) in going straight into a school on the south side of Chicago. I was fortunate that St. Brendan's was a school that really focused on education and spirituality. St. Brendan's was a Catholic school and church located half a block from my house. Being in Englewood in the 1970s was definitely different than being in Evanston. My new school was Catholic, which definitely helped with discipline. I attended St. Brendan's from third grade to eighth grade. All my classmates were blacks or Afro-Americans (terms we used in the 1970s to describe ourselves). Negro wasn't used too much by our community at this time unless you were more educated, more conservative, or an older adult of Dr. King's era.

Initially, I was teased about how I spoke because having mostly white classmates and teachers before meant that I talked like them. That was in Evanston, but this was Englewood. My classmates at recess teased "you talk white"; well, I did not "fight white". This means some of my classmates would "test me"—never in class, only at recess or before school. For the most part I held my own, and the other kids left me alone. I was fortunate to later have one of the biggest kids in class as a friend (Thanks, Calvin).

I also had a great third grade teacher, Sister Elizabeth Anne. She was enthusiastic, and she made learning fun. She also made the recommendation to my parents about me taking music classes after school. I did: first piano, then guitar, and later recorder. I don't play now, but music classes and preparing for recitals improved my concentration, drive, and discipline, and they gave me the ability to focus on long-range goals (the recital later in the year). My music teacher was Sister Mary Niemeyer. She was nice—if you were not taking music lessons. Her pushing and prodding helped me prepare for the recitals. I also learned about setting and achieving a goal.

The principal was Black/Afro-American (she even had a small Afro hairstyle). She was not "in" the Catholic Church. She was dynamic, educated, concerned about the children, the community and their self-image. Mrs. Brown, with her husband and three children, lived just around the corner, right across from St. Brendan's. It was uplifting and encouraging to see someone like her in a position of power and also living within the community. Just her sight encouraged me immensely. I must say after the "white flight" of the neighborhood, the church made an attempt to keep the parish/school stable during the transition of Englewood.

In addition to our standard lessons, there were these African American historical comic books. I learned on my own about Matthew Henson, Frederick Douglass, Harriet Tubman, Benjamin Banneker, and others in American history, as well as Toussaint in his overthrow/ rebellion against the French in Haiti and the famous Dumas family of France. I really enjoyed *The Three Musketeers* (both the story and the candy bar). The fact that that novel as well as others were written by a person of African Heritage gave me hope. To find out that Alexandre Dumas's father was a great officer in Napoleon's Army was quite fascinating. I also found out about one of Russia's great poets, Alexander Pushkin's African heritage, as well as the heritage of Beethoven and others. This increased my interest in history—to know that we were/are more than the descendants of slaves. I enjoyed all my classes, but history, especially black history, gave me hope for the future. The books by historian J. A. Rogers really opened my mind about black people worldwide and throughout all history. These books also improved my reading skills because I would read these books over and over again. It made me a better student overall.

Going to St. Brendan's helped me to focus and attain the basic skills that would help me to succeed in both high school and college. This school helped me with my identity as well. Although the majority of my teachers at St. Brendan's were white, I never felt that they did not have my best interest at heart—I never felt held back. I also felt encouraged to excel. These feelings gave me further confidence in education being a way out. I was an altar boy for a few years. I played football (not very well) for a few years. I played a few instruments and had a few recitals. What I really enjoyed was academics and the competition with my classmates.

I never saw Englewood as a bad neighborhood growing up (it was always home to me). I did feel that I had to leave so I could grow. When I was growing up in the neighborhood in the 1970s during summertime, we would play in the park until the street lights came on. We were kids, yet we felt safe. We were from the neighborhood. We rode our bikes, we played ball; and some time in my junior high years, tennis was introduced in the park district for youth (the National Junior Tennis League). My mom first played tennis a few years before with the nuns and played rather well. She encouraged me over the summer to play, so I played for Ogden Park, which was right across the street from my house.

It was so much fun. I took to it immediately. I would play for hours in the summer with an old Don Budge racquet that I found in my attic. Our team became quite good. We would play other parks in Chicago, as well as have them come to Ogden Park. I remember one year our team actually came in second in the city. We lost to Columbus Park on the west side. The winning team went to Ohio for the nationals.

One reason tennis appealed to me was it is an individual sport. It all depended on you (good or bad). I was also influenced by the fact that my mom played and my Uncle Wilbert, the professor at Chicago State University, also played. Uncle Wilbert had won a number of trophies that I saw in his home. I too would win a few trophies along the way— most valuable player as well as sportsmanship. I played throughout my summers in high school as well as the summer before college.

My parents always kept me busy, so I guess there was no time for mischief (or at least very little time). Another reason tennis was big at this time in the neighborhood was Arthur Ashe's prominence at this time. After he beat Jimmy Connor's at Wimbledon, it was hard to find a court; everyone and their mama wanted to play. I had to get up much earlier to play. Luckily, we lived across the street from the courts. Ogden Park was always the place to go, whether to play sports or just relax with my friends and relatives.

We lived next door to one of the last white families in the neighborhood. They would leave in the early 1970s. They initially came here from Germany before Hitler came to power. There was an older woman (old enough to be my grandmother), her middle-aged son, and her middle-aged daughter. There were two houses on one lot. The front one was the mother and son's. The back one was the daughter's. The older lady had a beautiful garden (an urban oasis) in the space between the two houses (as well as a statuette of the Virgin Mary). The older lady would introduce my mom to the Catholic Church in the late 1960s, I believe (I think the masses were in Latin. By the time I attended St.

Brendan's, the masses were in English). They were the best neighbors we would have at this address. The older lady piqued my mom's interest in gardening, although mom (as well as my dad) were knowledgeable about growing plants from living in the rural South. We would soon grow our own greens, tomatoes, okra, peppers, etcetera. I really enjoyed the older lady's radishes, which she gave me often. I was saddened when they moved only a few years after knowing them.

If there was one thing I could say about mom, it would be this: "If there was something she wanted to know about, she would pursue it wholeheartedly." She had an endless curiosity about things and life in general. She educated herself on many subjects, just like my dad. I would ask my parents numerous questions about things when I was in elementary school; so my father thought the *Encyclopædia Brittanica* would be a great investment.

One saying goes, "Be careful what you wish for." That was certainly the case with me. You see, they began to ask me to look up stuff for them, in addition to what I was already looking up. I did not mind because, back then, it was so much fun to have all this knowledge at my fingertips. Also, back then, information seemed more manageable (unlike now). The Encyclopedia definitely came in handy for school projects and to settle bets, much like how Google is used today. In the 1970s, the Encyclopedia was the final word (since we did not have computers).

I started writing poetry when I was ten. My mom made the mistake of telling me I was good, so I have been writing in one form or another since. It's amazing what a little encouragement can do. I was lucky to have it. I would even say I was blessed.

I remember my grandfather (father's father) Samuel Farnsworth Bethel dying when I was in eighth grade. It was my second semester. He lived in Covington, Tennessee at the time. I also remember my siblings: Dana, Sam, Dee, and our little brother Theodore Frederick, who was three years old. It was at this time I began to realize the influence of the Bethels in the community of Covington and the business interests my grandfather left behind in Covington, as well as the ones he once had in Chicago. Hearing/listening to these stories intrigued me. "What did/does it mean to be a Bethel?" People referred to my siblings and myself as "little Farns's kids." You see, my grandfather was Samuel *Farns*worth Bethel. Our father was Theodore *Farns*worth Bethel.

Our dad was "little Farns." If you grew up in the South, I'm sure you understand. It was ironic because dad was much bigger in stature than his father (at least six feet and two hundred pounds), yet he was "little Farns"

So many times when my siblings and I would be playing down in Covington, Tennessee, people would remark, "Those are little Farns's kids". I did not think much of it at the time, but I would later wonder what does being a Bethel mean, and its importance in this community of Covington, Tennessee.

Chapter Three

The time between graduating from St. Brendan's and going to high school was very eventful. My father took me with him to see my older brother Sam graduate from high school. I had visited with my siblings for about a month when I was ten and our little brother Ted was one. Teddy did not come when I visited Denver. This was the first time I would have an extended visit with my siblings and their mom Alice. I had a blast.

Now here I was again for my brother's graduation—also a blast. I always looked up to my brother Sam for his athletic ability and skills as a fisherman, hunter, and outdoorsman. He was and is a guy's guy or man's man. Post-graduation he would be a brick mason for a while and then an arborist in and around Denver. I was mostly a tagalong with the outdoor activities, but it was great to be with my older brother and dad. There was actually one hunting season in my junior year in high school where I got more pheasant when we were hunting (beginner's luck).

My father would tell a different story of me learning to shoot. I believe I was between ten and twelve. He and my brother were out and I was learning. Our dad gave me proper instruction on how to hold the weapon (12ga. shotgun I believe). I was wearing overalls (important). I slowly squeezed the trigger after I lined up the object (tin can in tree) with the site. Boom! My shoulder went back. Our father says the recoil popped my snap loose—I believe it was off before I shot.

I also remember fishing with my brother when I was ten in Denver. He was a great older brother. He would enter the work force and I would enter high school—goodbye to childhood.

With my thirst for learning and having such great teachers at St. Brendan, I was double promoted in junior high (more accurately, I spent the last few months of sixth grade with the seventh graders to see if I could do the work). My birthday is September 4, 1962, so I actually went through the registration process of high school while I was twelve. I believe I was thirteen during the first day of class. This was a closely-guarded secret. I did not need another reason to be possibly picked on. You see, I would be attending Quigley Preparatory Seminary South—what a mouthful—and what a great school it was. Sure, there were no girls (it was a seminary), but we had cheerleaders in wrestling and other sports from the all-girls Catholic schools in the area: Maria, Queen of Peace, Longwood, etc. I was focused, and dating was the farthest thing from my mind (at this time).

I really had an openness to priesthood throughout my four years at Quigley (although I downplayed it). I guess the other priests saw potential in me. What changed? Hormones. I still attended the neighborhood church of St. Brendan's, and the old priests there were pleased at my high school choice. We even had a Nigerian priest at St. Brendan. His name was Father Michael. Everyone in the family was concerned that I was going to become a priest, as if that was a bad thing. My parents were open to whatever I wanted. Quigley was a great way for the son of a working class person to get a great faith-based education (preferably going on to become a priest).

Today the school grounds belong to St. Rita, another Catholic high school that moved there from its other south side location. I guess Quigley closed because it was not producing enough priests, but I would argue they produced a lot of great people with conscientious motives (people who care). I would remember hearing about Pope John Paul II's visit in the fall of 1979, months after I graduated in May (just my luck).

I had a five-year hiatus from dealing with white students on a day-to-day basis. I was now at this college prep high school that was at least eighty percent white. It was not as big a culture shock as I had anticipated. My freshman year was the fall of 1975. There was a lot of racial tension in the Marquette Park area as African Americans wanted to move west of Western Avenue, which had been the dividing line for a while. I believe previously it was Damen Street. Quigley was on the west side of Western Avenue and the north side of Seventy-Ninth Street.

Due to the quality of teaching, and being a Catholic college prep school, we had people from all over Chicago and some suburbs. I went there for the academics, although I thought wrestling would be a practical sport (since they did not have boxing). I enjoyed the discipline of the sport. My parents hated when I was cutting weight. On more than one occasion, they threatened to pull me from the team. The other kids hated the running part but that was to endure the three-minute periods that would seem like forever. I would be on the wrestling team in three-and-a-half out of the four years I was at Quigley. I still remember the yelling of Coach Leonard Pero to this very day. You either liked him or you didn't, and he didn't care which one you chose. I liked him. He did not know I was also a good student. I surprised him and myself when I made National Honor Society (NHS), but I am getting ahead of myself. Let's go back to freshman year.

In most classes there were about two or three of us African Americans. Considering the racial tensions in the surrounding areas, I think the school did a great job to keep the students focused. The fact that it was also a Catholic school and college prep also kept us focused. Almost everyone there had their minds on college, the professions, the family business, technical training, and yes, the priesthood/seminary. For the most part we were focused. Beginning freshman year there were a few hundred of us; by senior year there were a little over a hundred (I think 113).

When I enrolled at this Catholic college prep institution, my parents were encouraging and for the most part let me explore. I tried out for a few sports. I was at that awkward age physically. I did not make soccer, but I did make the wrestling team. I did not try out for tennis because there was a conflict in seasons, and I thought wrestling would be more practical since boxing was not available. My first semester academically was a struggle, I only got one A and the rest Cs, Dad had a stern talk with me and said if the grades did not improve, I would be going to public school—not that there is anything wrong with public school. I just had reached a certain level at this time, and there weren't as many magnet schools—or access to them.

Since the school required some financial sacrifice on my parents' part, I totally understood that, as my dad put it, "You could get Cs at a public school." I gave a greater effort. I was very spartan in my social life, which is fitting because our mascot was the Spartans. I didn't have a social life, except for family gatherings. I had no real friends, just acquaintances at school. My focus was on school and wrestling. Although I did not wrestle much the first year, the time was well spent in gaining the endurance and strategy/knowledge that would help me in later years. The discipline helped me mentally and physically. When we had wrestling in gym class, I always won. This being said, I did not have too many troubles from my fellow students.

My grades improved as well as my skill in wrestling. I lettered both sophomore and junior years. I also would make it into the NHS. I still had limited social interaction with others outside of class. My focus was to get into a good college, validating my self-discipline.

From the time I graduated elementary school until the time I would go away to college, my family and I would spend our weekends during the summer constructing a house on a family property in Momence, Illinois, about fifty miles out of Chicago near Kankakee. My father was a third generation brick mason. My brother Sam, my cousins, and I dug the foundation with shovels. A neighbor and friend of my father poured the foundation and would do other concrete work later. I was taught how to make brick mortar by hand because the mixing machine broke. So for the great majority of the construction of this brick, ranch-style home, I made the brick mortar/cement.

The weeks that followed for that summer and the three summers following it would allow me to see a house erected from a foundation and to put roofing shingles on by hand with my mother and father. Yes, my mother helped as well, as she made sure we had healthy meals with a hot plate and slow cooker once we were able to get electricity hooked up from off the road.

My little brother Ted was three years old at the time. He played. He slept. He provided comic relief and helped when he could. This family project brought us together as a family, although there were times when tempers flared over timeliness in task completion, as well as over finances to continue the various stages of house building. The work on this house was hard physical labor, yet it prepared me to focus and stay on task to complete a job well.

The weekdays in the summer were spent playing tennis for Ogden Park. The physical labor in construction increased and so did my strength. My serves were more powerful and increased in speed. In wrestling, I was able to have greater physical control over my opponents. I was wiry, but my strength was increasing.

September arrived, and it was back to the books and wrestling. This cycle continued for three-and-a-half years. Although I was moving up in class rankings, by senior year I realized I did not have a date for our spring social. We could not call it a prom; I guess it had something to do with our institution being a preparation for the priesthood. At first I was not going to go. I got stiff resistance from my parents. I was not afraid of girls—in fact, the young ladies found me attractive as much as I enjoyed their company, and that was the problem.

I remember winning a dramatic match at a home meet and how the cheerleaders cheered. I felt really good that night, and after the meet, after putting away the mats and the halls were darkened and walking down the corridor, one of the cheerleaders came to me. She was slender, beautiful, and had a magnificent smile. She told me what a great match I had, embraced me, and kissed me. Her lips were soft and sweet. I did not even realize she wore braces. In wrestling, I definitely was not the best on the team, so this went straight to my head and other areas. Could I honestly be a priest, realizing what I was feeling and thinking at this time? She kissed me on the mouth—the softness and wetness of her lips was causing a great conflict. She was fifteen and I was fourteen (but she did not know this, nor would she ever find out). We never went out together. She was my first real kiss, yet the feelings and desires the kiss provoked would be problematic and made me ask myself: Was celibacy a realistic option for me?

Senior year came, and I did not have a clue who I would take to the spring social. The first young lady I asked had attended St. Brendan's with me. We graduated from eighth grade together. I asked her relatively early in senior year. I was really pumped up. She was bright. She was beautiful. She said yes. I was ecstatic. Nothing could go wrong. Nothing was further from the truth.

The truth was that at the end of the first semester, the young lady told me she could not go to the social with me. She would be unable to go because her class trip would overlap the day we would be going to my prom/social. She gave me the option that I could go to her prom. I had to decline. My ego was shattered. Whether the story was true or not, I felt let down. We never saw each other again.

The search was on for a new date. I noticed a young lady at my bus stop en route to Quigley. She attended CVS (Chicago Vocational School). I was so glad I had recently changed my bus route in going to school. We talked at the bus stop. First there was some hesitancy because she was so beautiful. I soon got over that as we built rapport with our conversations. She was reserved in public, yet very funny in private. She only lived a few blocks from where I lived. I met her parents. She met mine. I asked her. She accepted. We went to the prom/social. She was so beautiful (she also wore braces).

Our spring social happened on April 27, 1979. There were some snow flurries in the early evening. I was sixteen and she was eighteen (she also would never know my age). The theme of the prom was "Too Much Heaven"—how ironic. It was from an old Bee Gees song (the same guys that did the majority of the music for *Saturday Night Fever*, the movie that helped make disco mainstream). I was never too big on dancing, but I danced that night. It was magical and perfect until—until some classmates invited us to go to another party further north than the Palmer House (which is where we were). I asked my date. She agreed. Big mistake.

I took Lake Shore Drive and somehow got off on the wrong street. I did not realize the streets on the north side were different than the ones on the south side. On the south side, we had numbers and streets to make it easy to know what direction you were headed in. On the north side, it was just a series of names. If you were not familiar with the names (like me), you would probably get lost (like me). The south side was like the x-y coordinate system in math. The north side had angular and curved streets and a great deal more white people. I had never traveled to the north side before and I thought I was going to impress my date. At this point, I was sure the opposite was true. This was before cell phones and navigation systems existed. I was hopelessly lost. Being an African American in an unfamiliar neighborhood at this time in Chicago's history could've had a very negative outcome for me and my date. I figured if I could find a familiar street, then I could just head south—which is what happened. I found Halsted Street, and we kept going south until the numbered streets became more familiar.

I remember driving through the Englewood Concourse on Sixty-Third and Halsted. My friends and I would see martial arts movies on Saturdays in elementary school. I remember going to Sears, Woolworths, Montgomery Ward, and other popular shops at the time. I remember walking down Sixty-Third Street on Halsted and smelling the sweet, warm aroma of the Huck Finn donuts—oh what a treat to have one of those glazed donuts while waiting on an L train to take you to downtown Chicago. There was also this Chinese restaurant across from the Englewood movie theater where my buddies and I would sometimes buy almond cookies after the movie. Driving through this area on prom night made me realize how badly I would miss Englewood. This would be my last visit before college.

I remember bringing my date to her home and getting a kiss. That was my spring social of 1979. "Do You Think I'm Sexy" by Rod Stewart was one of the popular songs that night. I definitely wasn't feeling sexy. My date and I would see each other a few more times, but she had plans to go to her prom with someone else. She said this was promised before we ever started seeing one another. I took it the wrong way and we did not see each other until I gave her one of our prom pictures. Her parents were great and hated that we broke up. At this point, I was focused on finishing up high school and getting started with college.

Graduation day did come and I did make it into the upper 25 percent of my graduating class. Those who were in NHS wore their ribbon and medallion. My parents were so pleased. Graduation night was for them. Since my last name is Bethel, I was one of the first to receive my diploma; my family roared, and I smiled. All the years of hard work paid off.

Now I would be able to focus on the University of Illinois downstate in Urbana. Before that came the last summer of building the house and the last summer with the NJTL (the National Junior Tennis League). My Uncle Beverly would help with the house in the summer. His superb carpentry skills were greatly appreciated. My older brother Sam came from Denver to assist with putting the roof on the house. My sister Dee also helped with installing the electrical boxes for outlets in the rooms. The tail end of the summer was spent putting on the roof. It was a hot summer but a stark contrast to the brutal winter of senior year with record lows and snows.

Although I did not become a priest, I did internalize the emphasis on growth. The four areas of growth that were emphasized were (1) physical, (2) intellectual, (3) emotional, and (4) spiritual. I would definitely be challenged in all four areas throughout my life.

Chapter Four

I got great scores on the ACT. My composite was twenty-seven or twenty-eight. At this time these were great scores. My guidance counselor said he could get me in the Air Force Academy in Colorado. My parents thought differently. They had bad experiences of friends and family coming back from Vietnam, so I was talked out of it. Years later, I would became a Naval Officer—I guess you can't fight fate. Dad and I were having lunch downtown Chicago when I was college hunting, and he said, half joking and half serious, "What about Tuskegee (his alma mater where he earned his certificate in brick masonry)?" I didn't tell him no but that I would think about it. I knew how hard my parents worked, and this would be out of state. I thought about the costs, and so I declined.

I applied early admissions to the University of Illinois at Urbana-Champaign. I did not want to be limited to the courses that I would take so I entered regular admissions instead of the University's EOP (Equal Opportunity Program). I felt my ACT scores, grades, class rank, and extracurricular activities would be enough for me to get in. I also felt another minority person could have a chance. I was sixteen when we moved my things down to the U of I. It was my mom, dad, little brother Ted, and my cousin Fernando who helped me move in. I enjoyed the buzz of all the activity of students (freshmen) moving in for the very first time. I chose Allen Hall. There was a homey type of feeling. Allen Hall had a program called "Unit-One" where various artists, performers, activists, and celebrities would visit. Some would stay for a while, and others would actually teach classes/seminars on various topics. I remember meeting Paul Winfield, the actor (from the movie *Sounder* as well as numerous other movies), as well as Julian Bond, the activist and politician. There were numerous others I would meet.

Harold Washington came down when he was running for mayor. I also remember Dr. Margaret Burroughs's visit.

I worked all four years, first in food service to supplement the money my parents were able to provide. After sophomore year, when my parents told me that they could no longer afford to send me to school, I found a second job working as a computer operator at the Coordinated Sciences Lab.

My major was biology, pre-med (at least until the end of sophomore year). My biology grades were not great, which caused me to do some soul searching. I decided I would change my major—first, to political science, then to psychology.

I had taken entry-level general psychology in high school. I actually received college credit. I remember getting an A in the course. My Uncle Wilbert was also a professor of psychology at Chicago State University on the south side of Chicago. I believed if I could get my grades up, maybe I would go back to pre-med, but I also wanted to take entry-level business and computer classes since the 1980s were all about business and computers.

I remember the Iranians' takeover of our embassy as well as the Russians' going into Afghanistan. I also remember some anti-Iranian sentiment as well as an increased Christian presence on campus, especially groups seeking converts. Cults were also big at this time— think Moonies (Sun Myung Moon's Unification Church). I had a close friend who got into one of these cults whose parents had to kidnap her and have her deprogrammed. I never saw her again, although I heard through her brother, also a student, that she "got better." Reagan became president, and the hostages were freed. The campus became more conservative, more "Christian" (no relationship, just "coincidence"). There would be challenges to affirmative action nationally as well as challenges to the U of I to divest (since apartheid still existed) as well as to the United States.

The year 1982 was happy yet devastating for me. My great-grandmother Callie died at 104. She was the third wife of my great-grandfather Charles Henry. She received a personalized letter of congratulations from Pres. Jimmy Carter in 1977 when she turned 100. Speaking of politics, it was interesting to note the political support of people around her demographic. Many had been Republicans out of loyalty to Lincoln (who freed the slaves). With policies of Richard

M. Nixon (despite Sammy Davis Jr.'s initial support) such as "benign neglect," "tough on crime," and harassment, a number of the elderly/seniors would change their support, just like many southern Democrats changed to Republican with the passing and enforcement of the civil rights legislation.

I would really miss Mama Callie. I remember going over to her house when I was a child (she lived next door). She kept me when my parents were at work. I would also visit just to visit, and in addition, I would watch her as a teen as she increased in years. I would go over at the request of my Aunt Mentha, who she would end up living with. It was great to have an extended family. I was given the opportunity to appreciate the torch being passed from one generation to the next. The information/stories I gathered were priceless.

Her funeral was well attended by family and friends. The body was taken from Chicago to Covington, Tennessee via rail (Amtrak). The relatives were on the train with the body. I got off at the Champaign-Urbana stop to go back to school/work. Being an educator during her lifetime, I was sure she would want me to get back as soon as possible. It was the end of an era for me.

I was working two jobs now, so I had to get back to work. I worked in the dorm as a food service worker as well as a computer operator at an engineering lab on campus, mainly used by engineering students going on for advanced degrees. I remember connecting people to Wright-Patterson Air Force Base before the Internet. I remember some students working on AI (artificial intelligence). I remember being in a room of DEC PDP-10 computers (at first), then having a Vax unit or two in the room. It was as if someone took everything out of your living room, except for a chair. The C-programming language and Unix were becoming popular at an academic level. During the end of junior year, I knew I would be working over the summer at both jobs.

I was feeling uneasy about the future going into senior year. My father had experienced his first layoff at Republic Steel. He had been there for thirteen years. The United States was purchasing cheaper steel from abroad. Production was down. My father and others worked in teams to reline in brick, the containers used to transfer the molten steel. The brick in the cylinders would serve as a buffer/insulator to the container carrying the steel.

Republic Steel was on the southeast side of Chicago—very blue collar, very ethnic. I remember winning a wrestling match at St. Francis De Sales on the southeast side. This was fitting since when my father first arrived at Republic Steel as the first African American in the Masonry Department, he told me he had to literally fight on occasion for respect. He never lost. He also gained their respect and admiration as a person and craftsman, a craft that he learned from his father who learned from his father which was honed at Tuskegee, where my father got his masonry certification. I am sure he had experience working for his dad and Uncle Thomas (who was also a brick mason). In the late 1960s, there was a lot of prejudice/resistance to hiring African Americans in the trades. My father's co-workers were Poles, Germans, other Slavs, and other whites. Ironically, I am named after a Pole, Tony Socialowski, who got my father the job at Republic Steel. Life is strange. I would see many of these men at my father's funeral.

Speaking of funerals, on August 1982, I was excited to start my senior year. I would be twenty the following month. I worked this summer (as the last two) down in Urbana. This summer, I worked and lived with friends off campus. I would then receive a phone call from my father telling me my Uncle Beverly had passed.

My great Uncle Beverly also worked with my grandfather and Uncle Thomas, but he was a carpenter. He would become a master carpenter and contractor in Chicago. He also lived in Englewood down the street from us. He did a great deal of the carpentry work on the house we built in Momence, Illinois, from 1975 to the house completion in 1979. Uncle Beverly died from complications of cancer. I remember my uncle as a Renaissance man. He was a former teacher, coach, as well as an excellent cook. I remember his great spaghetti being in demand at family gatherings. I remember him coming over numerous times to help with family functions, sometimes staying the night. He would often tell me quotes of famous people in history. I could not believe he was now dead.

Up to this point I was doing quite well, especially professionally. Over the past summer, I gained admittance to a rigorous internship program offered by the University of Illinois. It was called the Administrative, Higher and Continuing Education (AHCE) Internship. I was fortunate to land a position as an intern in the business office of the U of I in the Department of Data Processing.

I would work with Mr. P. R. Das. He was very well-respected in his field/department. He was also Indian and much darker than me. I thought it was ironic that my great-great-great-grandmother would have a Hindi name (Nidra), and here I was with an Indian boss.

I was also accepted into an organization that would help senior minorities connect with jobs and grad schools. This organization was called the Minority Student Advisory Committee (MSAC). We would be responsible for (with a little help from faculty) getting different corporations, graduate schools, as well as other organizations to come to our conference. The conference would take place in the spring of 1983, a month or so before my own graduation.

With the exceptions of the two deaths (Mama Callie, then Uncle Beverly), things seemed to be going well, although somber. I routinely began my work and classes, then something happened in October that would be like a knockout punch. My father died. It was totally unexpected. He was forty-seven. I received the phone call in the middle of the night from my mom. My roommate answered, then slowly gave me the phone. My mom said, "He's dead, he's dead." She was crying. I asked, "Who? Who is dead?" dreading the words that I already knew, yet needed to hear. She said "your father," and then she gave me details that I was barely able to hold on to.

I made arrangements with the university to leave. I went home to help with the funeral and my little brother who was ten years younger than me (ten at this time). I remember going into his room after getting home from the bus station, and I received a bear hug and some tears. Did that mean I was the man of the house now? I barely knew what I was going to do next, much less how to help my mom and brother.

I know it sounds selfish, but my intentions were to leave as soon as possible after graduation. This was a place you retired to or a place you raised your kids or a place where you did agricultural work. It was not a place for me, fresh out of college looking for a future, especially since we did not have a family business. I had to get it together. My siblings from Colorado would come over soon. I would have to be strong for all of us. I believe I put all this extra pressure on myself. I could not shake the emptiness. I wanted the degree for him, a reward/appreciation of those long, hot hours in the steel mill.

Although he got his certificate in brick masonry from Tuskegee, I found out he had dreams of becoming an architect. I always wanted to do something special (academically) for him and my mom since they sacrificed so much and worked so hard and were great role models. I always wanted to do well for them. Now my father was dead—before he turned fifty.

After my father's funeral, I was in a fog of emotion. My little brother Teddy took his grief out on the football field and did quite well in my father's absence at least superficially. My mom was met with resistance if the talk revolved around feelings. I guess it was through football he could stay connected with Dad. You see, Dad helped out often with the team and would get an award (posthumously) for his service. This meant a lot to me because Momence (back then) was very conservative and white. There were only three or four black kids on the team. My brother Teddy was the fastest of them all. He played football from the time he was eight to eighteen. He built a great reputation as a running back, and would later graduate from Bishop McNamara High School in Kankakee, Illinois.

My father (and mother) both experienced overt racism during their lives, yet my father was a fair man. He enlisted the help of some whites when building our home in Momence. He would walk my (then) sister-in-law Roxy down the aisle to marry my brother Sam. He loved their little boy Tony, who was named after me—how humbling. He remarked to me later after the wedding, "Now I can die." How prophetic. You see, Roxy was white and it did not matter to my father. He could not love his grandchild any more than he did. My father believed in giving everyone the benefit of the doubt regardless. In fact, I was named after a white guy that got my father his job at Republic Steel. Times had definitely changed from the late 1960s to the early 1980s. Not all the whites my father spoke about from his childhood were racists. They did (outwardly) follow the conventional behavior that was expected of them. I would find out many did good deeds on the side or behind closed doors.

I remember one particular story that wasn't so positive, and was one of my reasons to travel to all seven continents and see all seven oceans.

My father and his father (grandpa) were traveling up north (Chicago) to see family in the mid 1940s. In Cairo, Illinois (going north), you could sit where you wanted on the bus, and my father (who was a boy at this time) did. Going up north was fun, and visiting relatives and family and friends even more so. Going to different sites in Chicago was quite exciting. It was quite an eventful summer.

The summer ended, and then there was the bus ride to go back to Covington, Tennessee. In Chicago, my father sat where he pleased. As the bus was about to leave Cairo, Illinois, to head south across the Mississippi River, my grandpa gently reminded him, "You are not up north anymore," which meant that he couldn't sit where he wanted. I am sure it must have been a painful thing to tell your child (especially a black male). I say "especially a black male" because black males have been in (and died in) every major war this country has had for the freedom of others while not being free themselves.

What is so important is that we never gave up. We never gave up on ourselves nor our country. We have to remember it took many different people to elect our first African American president, and we are also fortunate that we live in a country that allowed Mr. Obama to take office. Now if they would trust him to lead. We as a people never gave up hope, always had faith, and made the best of situations.

When my father died, I did not give up hope, but it was as if the wind had left my sails and I lost my rudder, both at the same time. I felt dead in the water. I had no direction, and others were expecting me to step it up when I did not even have a clue (I was faking to keep others strong).

I muddled through senior year emotionally but professionally— it was quite successful. As a Minority Student Advisory Committee (MSAC) board member, we (with the help from the staff) made our conference the most widely attended conference in recent years. Other corporations took notice, and I had on-site interviews. I was offered a position as a manager trainee for Jewel Foods (which at the time, considering the economy, was not a bad deal). I felt like I needed something in the present that would pay rather than going to another school that would take money. I also felt that with graduation around the corner and my mom and brother back home, I had to do something responsible. I tried to think what my dad would want me to do, and how could I be the greatest help to the family.

I also interviewed for a job at the U of I in data processing in the business department. I did not get the job because they were looking for a different minority (a woman). I heard through friends (or this is the story I was told). Either way, I was not mad, because I had found a job. Continental Bank also turned me down for data processing. So (for now) computers were not in my immediate future. Since there were a little over 3 percent African Americans at the U of I at this time, I couldn't beat myself up too badly (I believe its 6 percent now, thirty years later) I started at Jewel a couple of weeks after graduation (my choice). I wanted to get started doing something—contributing.

Graduation was great. My Uncle Wilbert and Aunt Mentha came, as well as Aunt Hertha, and even Aunt Katie from Covington. There was my little brother Teddy and my cousin Shavonne who was between three and four. Shavonne was my cousin Wanda's child, and Wanda was Uncle Beverly's first born. Shavonne would be brilliant at school. Earning money through child modeling, she would attend HBCUs (Historically black colleges and universities), gaining a BS then an MS in Chemical Engineering. She would go on to Proctor & Gamble where she is now Global Oral Care R&D Section Head. When I see Pro-Health/Crest products, I think of her. I interviewed with Proctor & Gamble senior year (I did not get it). I am so pleased with Shavonne.

Graduation was truly my day, and my relatives were so proud. I put a brave front, but inside I was empty. I had no desire to move back home. I did not even know if I wanted a job in business, but I knew I had to soldier on. I did know my mom and little brother needed me. I did know that bills needed to be paid. I did know that I did not want to let anyone down. I had a job in a tough economic time—during the early 1980s and fresh out of college. What the hell was I whining about? I worked two jobs to put myself through. I was a black male with no children, no criminal record, no drama. Why was I feeling empty?

I worked at a Jewel in Joliet, Illinois. The manager that trained me, Bill, was a great, patient guy. Diane and Michelle were responsible for the operations of the store. I started as a cashier then went behind the front desk to learn the day-to-day operations from Diane and Michelle. They were fast, yet patient. Almost all the employees were white (with the exception of a bagger and another person further along in the trainee process than myself). I attended college with many whites (it was the U of I), but the whites here were working class, having problems similar to my working class neighborhood growing up. It was definitely more conservative. It seemed just white, not ethnic like Chicago.

The most interesting part of my job was the drive from Momence to Joliet via the back roads and back home again. Why was I so bored? Isn't this what we go to college for—to get a job and settle down? I was only twenty, and it had only been a few weeks, but I knew I did not want this life. Worse than that, I knew I could not sustain this facade. I had a feeling it would eventually crumble, and it did. My mom and brother tried to keep my spirits up; I should have been there for them. My mom had a little bit of savings, but there was no insurance. My brother still attended Catholic school. I helped as much as I could, but I was dying inside. We lived in a very rural, economically-depressed area outside of town. This was not the plan I envisioned, but I had to keep going. The parents took turns carpooling the kids into town to the local Catholic school.

My brother had his bouts of dealing with the other students, especially after losing Dad. Later he would open up and tell me the other kids were picking on him. Most of his aggressive behavior was contained on the football field, where he helped the Momence Vikings secure a few local championships as running back.

By August, I knew I had to go. Only a few months after graduation, I had to free myself, regardless of the consequences. I kept telling myself I was doing this for the good of the whole family. I reasoned if I lost control, that would be another obligation/tragedy that my mom would have to deal with.

I decided I would join the navy.

Chapter Five

I wanted out of this rural community. I had nothing against it. It just was not for me—at least for now. I was not ready to settle down yet. Wild oats needed to be sown. I know I was not a good son or brother. The problem was I did not know what I was. I always just went to school and did what I was supposed to do. Now was the rebellion—at the most inopportune time. I reasoned if I did something that I loved, it would soften the blow, especially if I was successful.

I talked to the recruiter initially, and I was going to go into data systems early February 1984. This would give me a chance to enhance those basic computer skills I learned plus learn about electronics. This would be a great opportunity for me after college—hands-on experience.

I hated letting the people down at Jewel. I hated leaving before I had a chance to prove myself (especially being a minority male). I was hoping my success in the military would vindicate me. My recruiter subtly said, "You should take the Nuclear Qualification Test since your ASVAB (the military SAT) scores are so high." I took the test and passed. I second-guessed myself and would be attending Nuclear Power School in Orlando next year, but boot camp would be next month—a few weeks after I turned twenty-one. They say "pride goeth before the fall," and I would fall hard.

It was the night before I was going to Great Lakes, Illinois. I stayed at the Congress Hotel and roomed with someone else who was going to serve in the coast guard. Morning came soon enough, and I got indoctrinated into the taste of military food. Later that day, after all the paperwork would be completed at the Chicago enlisted processing center, I got on the Chicago Northwestern Train and headed to Great Lakes, Illinois, RTC (Recruit Training Command).

I would be the first person in the family I knew of that would be going to the navy. Everyone before me had gone to the army or the air force. Many had said the navy was prejudiced. I guess it was because of the racial tensions/violence on the ships, especially as recent as the 1960s and 1970s. I had to find out for myself. Although I would say for myself things overall would be positive, there were struggles—not racial.

As I was walking towards the base with its guards and wire fence, I thought of the saying "Join the navy, see the world." I was the first of my company (group) to arrive. I had my own personal escort to the mess hall. He was in uniform and a senior recruit. He gave me tips on how to survive. He was past service week ("hell week") so he knew he would be leaving soon. I tried to absorb everything he was saying. I was in my civilian clothes. I could not wait for my uniform. The chow was hearty full of carbs and meat. I tried to ask as many questions as he would allow based on what I heard from my recruiter. On the way back to the barracks, we practiced some marching to the tune of "Anchors Aweigh." He was white, and he didn't seem prejudiced to me.

I was still the only one from my company, so I was set in the office with some senior enlisted personnel. I felt a little uneasy because I had a feeling their feelings would be changing towards me as soon as more recruits arrived to make up our company. It was now nighttime, and as we went into the night, a steady stream of folks in their civilian clothes would enter the barracks. It was at this point I was put in with the others. I knew this would be it for the next several weeks—no yelling yet, but it was coming. The ordeal of boot camp would soon begin. I was reminded of that uneasy yet exciting feeling that you get when the roller coaster first goes to the top and you haven't dropped yet, but you know it's about to go down—and it did, at 4:30 a.m., when the DI (drill instructors) came in and said, "Get the f--- out of those mother f------ racks (beds)!"

Empty trash cans were rolled around. The noise got your attention—you wanted to get up to get away from the noise. Hurriedly we got up and got dressed in the clothes we came with. We were put in groups and marched off to chow. The other uniformed recruits glanced, and some smirked as if to say "Welcome to Great Lakes." Marching to the chow hall was hilarious (although not at the time)—trying to walk in time, stepping on the other person's feet because no one knew how to march yet.

Over the next few days, we would be measured for and receive our uniforms. We would also be poked and prodded, receive a variety of shots, have blood samples taken, receive glasses, have dental work done, as well as exercise and march, march, march! We would be mashed (it had nothing to do with the movie or TV series); it meant *make a sailor hurt*). Although I was in decent condition, it could be quite challenging to lie on your face, with arms and legs extended, holding the contraction for several seconds for numerous repetitions. Every weekend, we would compete with other groups/companies to see who the best was athletically and who marched the best. Various drills and inspections focused on "attention to detail."

As the weeks passed, we jelled as a unit, performing drills with precision and learning the value of teamwork and camaraderie. We would have discussions amongst ourselves during break time known as "coke and smoke." These breaks were few and brief, but we would find out we were from all across the United States, from coast to coast, as well as Guam and Puerto Rico. We were from the coasts, from the North, South, East, and West. We were truly an American force to be reckoned with LoL (Land of Lincoln—I'm from Illinois). We had all shades and numerous ethnic groups.

Around the fifth week in, we reached something called "hell week" where we had to do service work in the galley for the hundreds of recruits and staff at Great Lakes. The work was grueling, though ironically not for me. We all were designated certain positions—mine was Galley Yeoman. We kept records and we marched our companies over at 3:30 a.m. (I think) and at night—way after the galley closed. For a week, we did not see the sun unless we had an opportunity to leave the galley, which was rare. The others were responsible for food preparations, serving, cleanup, and sanitation of the galley and cookware for all three meals for hundreds every single day. March home, and in a few hours, march over again. You worked hard yet learned the value of service and humility.

After the end of the week, we were relieved and received our coveted white hats. We now looked like real sailors and not "raisin heads" (which is what we were called because we were only allowed to wear our black watch caps before). We were now the senior class. We walked taller, and we moved with precision in time. As we looked at the new recruits, we too would smile, thinking, "Welcome to Great Lakes."

At this point, we could see the light at the end, and it wasn't the train. We often talked amongst ourselves about our reasons for joining. For some, it was money for college. For others, it was family military tradition. Others needed direction. Others wanted a challenge. Some had nothing better going on in their lives. Some had to escape the law. Some wanted to get training on specific equipment so they could get a better civilian job. Me, I guess I came to find myself. Having a degree in psychology, all this fascinated me. The different motivations got my interest. I remember the Mormons from Utah doing their service work. I remember one white guy from Texas who was kicked out of his house because he would not stop seeing his black girlfriend.

We all had our motives. Having a degree in psychology, others wanted to know why I did not try for the position of officer. I did not feel it would be right to be a leader over people had I not gone through what they had. My company respected that, but they still thought I was crazy. Maybe I was.

Throughout boot camp, we would have various classes on basic healthcare, navy rules and regulations, seamanship, etc. We would also take written tests, as well as a physical training test before we could graduate. I thought of the Latin motto of Quigley, "Ora Et Labora" (prayer and work), and the four types of growth (physical, intellectual, emotional and spiritual). All these areas were tested in boot camp and in my years in the military overall. Having performed well on all my tests, we had a vote amongst ourselves based on who we felt epitomized military bearing, leadership, teamwork, camaraderie. I voted for someone else. The results really surprised me. It was me. I was voted "Honor Man" of company 272. You do not know how much this meant to me. This group of diverse fellows from all over the United States, Guam, and Puerto Rico voted for me, an African American from Englewood. The majority of my company was white. There were no racists here. I felt pride for the south side. My name would be mentioned at graduation, and my family would be able to sit at a special area.

I guess having knowledge of psychology/human behavior benefitted me. I understood the concept of taking everything away to make everyone equal and slowly giving back privileges based on merit. It wasn't rocket science, but maybe I had an advantage, at least psychologically. I did not feel advantaged when the drill instructor was in my face screaming and hollering for some small infraction, but it is attention to detail that keeps a ship afloat, whereas a loss of attention could sink it. I don't think the modern recruits have to deal with that. I don't believe my daughter had to deal with it (as badly) when she went to Great Lakes more than twenty years later.

Graduation day came. My family came from the south side of Chicago. They were pleased. They were impressed by the polished marching and drills and to hear my name being announced as "Honor Man" of company 272. We had a great feast at the Ponderosa/Bonanza or some steak chain. The meal was much better than boot camp chow. I was in my sailor suit and white hat, almost like the guy on the Cracker Jack box—except I was black.

My family seemed very proud. I was the first to be in the military in my family since my Great-uncles Thomas and Beverly. I was the first navy man.

I had little time for R&R. I reported back to Great Lakes but to the Naval Training Center (NTC). I would go to Machinist's Mate class "A" (MM "A") school and a temporary duty before going to Orlando, Florida. At MM "A" school, we learned about piping systems, hydraulic theory, and pump and valve repair. Piping repair was very hands-on. It was a nice switch from college, and it reminded me of when I worked on the house with my dad.

After passing my tests, I was placed at Great Lakes Detention Facility—not as a prisoner, but to work. It was a temporary holding area/jail. It was almost always empty. The Master At Arms operated out of the building. Fridays and Saturdays could get busy in breaking things up, but rarely were there more than two people behind bars simultaneously. It usually would be one, and they would usually be released to their command the next day.

Things were going along steadily, and I wanted to go to downtown Chicago for Memorial Day. It was the height of the break dance craze in the 1980s, and I wanted to see a movie called **Breakin** at the Chicago Theatre. I did not have any idea I would meet my future wife there— definitely not in line going into the movie theater. Cynthia was there with her friend and their siblings. I noticed her in line but did not say anything because the line was moving and she and her friend had an eye on their siblings. I lost track of them when I stopped for popcorn. Ironically, when I went into the darkened theater, I sat down next to Cynthia (my future wife). We laughed at the same time during the movie and would make side comments to one another. Later in the film, I asked her for her phone number. I had nothing to write with. She happened to have something to write with and gave me her number. We agreed to meet the next week I was off at the same time and same theatre.

Going to the next date, the weather was dreary, overcast, rainy, and chilly. The only bright spot would be I would be seeing Cynthia—or so I thought. I had bought some expensive chocolate-covered almonds since this was our first official date. The weather was so rainy I decided to visit a deli next door to the theater for shelter and for a bite to eat. The rain kept pouring down, and the time continued to pass—no Cynthia. I recounted in my mind if the instructions I had given were clear. Did I make a mistake?

After about a half-hour to forty-five minutes, I began to become concerned. I used a payphone (it was 1984) to call her. She was also upset because her mom would not let her see me. I knew that she was old enough (she was nineteen and I was going on twenty-two), so what was wrong? Although she was nineteen, she stayed on the south side with her mother and siblings. She worked downtown at Northwestern in the telecommunications department, yet she lived at home, and that meant she lived by her mom's rules. One of her mom's rules states no dates unless Mom saw who she was going out with. When she told this to me, I was angry of course, but I had to respect her mom, considering the neighborhood she was from and the negative stereotype about sailors. So I thought about it for a moment and decided to try this again. After scheduling another date—this time, we would go to her home first and see her mom—I ate half the chocolates and threw the rest away. I went back to Great Lakes.

The next time, I went to her mom's house after getting on a bus, after leaving the train station from downtown Chicago. She lived in a secure building on Thirty-fifth and Rhodes. It was a secure building with security and a log to sign in. I met with her mother, and we talked, and we talked, and we talked. She did not seem like such a bad person. In fact, Doris (her mom's name) and I hit it off rather well. Cynthia and I were both happy about that. We went out on our date, and that would be the procedure while I saw her in Chicago. I would visit, and then we would go somewhere via public transportation, since I did not have a car at Great Lakes. Time seemed to fly; our dating had definitely made my stay at Great Lakes more tolerable.

Midsummer came, and it was time to go to Orlando, Florida. I said my goodbyes to my family and to Cynthia and leapt into the unknown. Nuclear Power School was interesting in that I got along well with my instructors, although my performance was not all that great. I should have breezed through this program given my background and test scores. I studied, but it was the pace the information was coming at. This was not college. There was no time to ponder information. You had to process the information given at the pace it was given. I knew I wasn't stupid. It was the pace and the format. This was the military. I should have known better. I went to every class, yet I felt as if I was sinking in quicksand—the more I struggled, the faster I would go down.

We had an apartment-like setting on base, and they really tried to give it a college feeling but I just wasn't "getting it" as fast as the tests were coming. The instructors empathized, but what could they do? I went to extra hours for study. My only duty right now was to learn this material, so why was I failing? The instructors knew I was trying. I was not the only one. We were all on extra study hours. There were all colors and all backgrounds represented. I got a small comfort in this. The variety proved it wasn't a race thing. No superiority, no inferiority—we were all represented, we were all struggling looking for help. I only kept getting further behind, and my GPA kept slipping and slipping. Finally, it was over. I felt like a failure—again.

If there was a bright spot (if it could be called that), it was that those students that seemed worthy and who had put forth great effort—and who the instructors thought were worthy—were offered the opportunity to volunteer for Submarine Service. I volunteered in a heartbeat. I had to vindicate myself. Although this meant going to another school, I was definitely motivated to prove my instructors made the right decision. The submarine force was all volunteer—a group of motivated men.

I did not want my fate to be that of a friend of mine who stopped trying and got a "bad attitude. The navy put him on an oiler. I always wondered what had happened to him. I had known him since just after boot camp at Great Lakes. Other more difficult drops followed him. I did not want this fate or some type of negative discharge from the navy like bad conduct or dishonorable. I was an "Honor Man"—I had to get my honor back. Going to submarine school seemed to be a way to redeem myself.

The school was in Groton, Connecticut. This would be my first trip to the Northeast, and I would be driving up with a friend up to Connecticut. It was the fall, and the colors of the leaves caught my eye. The base was very scenic. The instruction was very real. Submarines fascinated me, and I wanted to learn more about them. I also enjoyed the surrounding area when I was not in class. I remember seeing a popular movie called **The Terminator** with Arnold Schwarzenegger. I saw the movie with some buddies. I definitely felt that I was back. I had planned to get engaged to Cynthia when I got back to Chicago.

The weeks flew by. There was this one daunting test called the wet trainer that we would have to endure. It was a mock-up of various pipes and small to larger holes that had to be plugged up with various materials using a patch kit we were trained to use earlier. Water came out at various pressures, and the water felt like ice water. Our class was broken up into two groups with two different mock-ups. Our group did well—we were not perfect, but at least we stopped the flooding before the water got above the deck plates (flooring in the engine room). We passed. I passed my written examinations.

As a group, the class went to Mystic Seaport in Mystic, Connecticut. It was a fun time. I received my orders to go to another school in Charleston, South Carolina, before I would go to my submarine (USS **M. G. Vallejo** SSBN 658). This final school was very job-specific and gave an overview of some of the equipment I would be working on, as well as tools and procedures that were used.

I would first go to Chicago to spend time with Cynthia and my mom and brother. My mom was not pleased at me wanting to get engaged; in fact, she was dead set against it. "You are just twenty-two. You are too young," she said. I was so determined. This was the first time I defied my mom about something major. Neither she nor I liked it. Prior to my relationship, I was the ideal son and held up as an example to my little brother. When I was adamant about getting engaged over my Christmas vacation and getting married later in 1985, my mom was livid (to say the least). I loved Mom, and I loved Cynthia, but I would not choose one over the other, yet I was still determined to get married.

Cynthia and I would spend a couple of days downtown at the Hotel Intercontinental on Michigan Avenue. My buddies and I had spent a few weekends here when we had come from Great Lakes to have a night out. It had a great atmosphere and was military-friendly in price and attitude. During the day, Cynthia and I would shop for and get an engagement ring on Jewelers Row on Wabash Street. The nights were spent talking and ordering room service.

The Christmas vacation, then New Year's, was over much too soon. It was now 1985, and soon time to report to my first ship.

Chapter Six

The adventure was about to begin. To a young male in his twenties, this was ideal. I thought about movies like ***Das Boot*** (The Boat) and ***The Hunt for Red October***, movies that would later become classics. The reality was not quite as glamorous, but the teamwork, camaraderie, and positive attitudes (for the most part) were real. We were a tight-knit group of professionals working together. We would get our ship (Mariano G. Vallejo SSBN 658) ready for sea trials. We had just taken the ship over from the gold crew (we were the blue crew). There is always a turnover period between the crews, between patrols, so one group knows the condition of the ship and what needs to be done in preparation for the next cruise. Once we got the turnover from the other ship and once the captain was satisfied, there would be a small change of command ceremony symbolizing the turnover, making it official. It was now time to get our vessel ready for sea trials.

Sea trials are where we tested the sub at various speeds, angles, and depths. It was like test-driving a car—but even more dangerous. If something was not stowed (stored) properly (i.e., tools or equipment), it could very easily become a projectile to damage the ship or a crew member.

There was a submarine qualification I had to study for and pass: first a written exam, then a board of qualified submariners onboard asked you a series of questions to determine if you were knowledgeable enough. On submarines, since it was a small crew in such a dangerous environment (the submerged pressure and depth intensified any flooding, fire, or damage control scenario), everyone had to know a little bit about everyone else's equipment just in case they were nearby when the casualty started. There were times when *you* had to act and did not have time to get someone.

You had to pass your submarine qualifications to stay onboard submarines. You were given two patrols to do this. Some advanced people finished in one patrol (I was so close). I wanted more time to "know it" this was not information you could just "pump and dump." Your knowledge secured the life next to you. Your ignorance put that life (as well as your own) in jeopardy. Our rotation was three months away from Charleston (our home port) and three months in Charleston for training and R & R (rest and relaxation).

In August of 1985, I would marry Cynthia in Chicago. It was an outdoor wedding with my family from Chicago, my mother and brother, along with my siblings from Colorado (Sam, and Dee). My great-aunts Hertha and Mentha were there, as well as my uncle Wilbert, a professor of psychology at Chicago State University who did the extensive research of the Bethel family in North Carolina and Tennessee. There was also my mom's mom (Bernice) who we called "ma" (pronounced "muh"). This was a family reunion of sorts; since my time in the military, I had a very limited meeting with any of these folks, up to and including my wife Cynthia.

The wedding was at Cynthia's best friend's house. The maid of honor and preacher were late. The wedding was very late (are they ever on time?). It was hot outside, humid, August in Chicago. None of this mattered to me because I was in love, and my bride looked radiant. The maid of honor and preacher finally arrived. My best man was Cynthia's brother, Glenn. The remainder of the day went off without a hitch.

We would go on a cruise to the Bahamas. This time, though, I would be above the water (not below it). The cruise was fun. We had a great time on our honeymoon soaking up the sun and having fun shopping for souvenirs. The honeymoon was over much too soon, and we were now at her mother's house on the south side of Chicago.

I had to get ready mentally to go back since I had such a great time on my break. I actually had mixed feelings of going back, but duty was duty, married or not. It was back to Charleston, South Carolina, and the barracks, until it was time to be bused to our submarine in Kings Bay, Georgia. I was positive about it—I could be flying overseas to go to Holy Loch in Scotland (which wasn't too bad, I heard).

I qualified submarines early in my second patrol. I was now working full-time in my division. Earlier on the first patrol, I had to spend my time in the galley (chow hall) helping out because I was the junior person in my division. Each division had to send someone at some point, so I and a few other hapless souls went (I guess this makes up for that cushy job I had as a recruit at Great Lakes). We did well while counting the days until we would go back to our divisions.

I was a machinist mate in the auxiliary (A) division, one of the more macho divisions. We had equipment fore (front) and aft (back) of the submarine and in every compartment: hydraulics, compressed air, refrigeration, industrial gases, plumbing and damage control, atmosphere control, and any gray-area fix-it type of jobs. I had my eyes set on atmosphere control and making the ship's oxygen using the oxygen generators, but for now I worked on gage calibration and kept the hatches (doors) on the submarine in working order and watertight. I took these jobs very seriously. Our lives depended on it.

I would receive two letters of commendation for my work later. In the off time of the next patrol, I attended some advanced training schools like atmosphere control equipment. The great prize was oxygen generator school. The school was a few weeks long, and you had to pass a written and a practical—one on one with the instructor, where a fault was programmed in the machine and you had to solve it. This is one of the most complicated pieces of equipment that an auxiliary division ("A" ganger) would deal with. There were ten of us in the class. I was the only black man in the class. One person failed. I barely passed, but now I could work on the coveted oxygen generators, as well as the CO_2 scrubbers and CO burners.

I worked hard to understand the theory and reached a level where I was one of the submarine qualifiers for atmosphere control equipment. I enjoyed the challenge and extra work in order to help my fellow crew members. My evaluations were running at a 4.0 level (4.0 being the highest). Various upper-level personnel kept prodding me about becoming an officer (since I already had a bachelor's degree), but internally I did not feel it yet.

The year was 1987, and Cynthia was pregnant with our first child. I was on schedule to go back to Great Lakes, Illinois for diesel engine school. I made a request to the command to stay back so that I could help with the baby since she had not given birth yet. Luckily, there was someone in the division that volunteered for the position, so I stayed behind to help with my first child.

I walked with Cynthia for a long time on July 4, thinking our child would be born on that day. It would not be. My daughter, Brianna Ariel, would be born the next day on July 5. This was also a good and fitting day because my mom was born on December 5 and my youngest brother was born on March 5, so I guess the fifth day of the month is good for me. Brianna had a head full of hair. She was beautiful (they are all beautiful, especially when they are yours).

Now my wife could eat pizza, whereas when she became pregnant she hated pizza (one of her favorite foods). She also had a craving for a Jamoca Almond Fudge Shake from a fast food chain not too far from the house. Cynthia was such a good mom and very enthusiastic about breastfeeding and other motherly duties.

We were proud parents enjoying our daughter, then one day, a few weeks/months later, Brianna began to have a seizure while her mother was holding her. We knew our daughter was not well. We called 911, and our daughter was taken to the naval hospital first, where she was diagnosed with a mild case of rickets. After she was diagnosed, she was transferred to the Medical University of South Carolina (MUSC) for further treatment. Her mother stayed with her the whole time. My sub had returned by now. We found that there were certain nutrients our daughter was lacking. She was given supplements for a few days to strengthen her body. Members from my ship brought cards and toys. These guys were great! They asked if there were any additional ways that they could help. I feel they had done enough to allow me to miss a patrol to help take care of my family. I never will forget that.

Knowing that my family was safe, I threw myself back into my work with renewed energy. Brianna got much better and so did my evaluations—I was a 4.0 sailor (the highest rating in evaluations). I had qualified for the highest watch station for my division, which was atmosphere control watch. I was also helping others become qualified in submarines. I felt like I was making a contribution. I thought this was the time—the time to attempt officer training. My evaluations had been a continuous 4.0. I had the approval of senior enlisted personnel, as well as the officers onboard. I got my packet (paperwork) signed off and sent off via personnel.

Months passed for the reviewing process, and life went on as usual. Other senior personnel said I would not get it on the first try and I should just be patient. I figured I did all that I could do with the paperwork.

All the t's were crossed and all the i's were dotted. All I could do was wait and continue to work onboard the sub.

When I had the opportunity, I asked others about Officer Candidate School (OCS) in Newport, Rhode Island. I asked for pointers on what to prepare for and how. No one seemed to have any direct answers about how I should prepare and the curriculum there. I remember going home and going through the mail. The letter arrived. Was it acceptance or was it denial? The only way to find out was to open it. I said a silent prayer and opened the letter. My prayers were answered. I was accepted to OCS in Newport, Rhode Island. Praise God!

I would be the first black officer (that I knew of) in the family (at the time). I had a white family member that was a confederate officer, but I did not research that for obvious reasons. Although the family was very proud, I was still apprehensive about the curriculum and being prepared for it. How was officer training different from enlisted boot camp? I would soon find out.

Cynthia, Brianna, and Cynthia's sister moved back to be around family near Chicago. After driving them up and after a brief stay, I went to Newport. I soon found out about the yelling and screaming upon arrival. The yelling was just as loud, if not more so. In this case, it was mostly our seniors that were doing the yelling (no profanity). We had one chief per battalion, and they were stern, but the person that would be in your face was a senior personnel (one of your own). Only the first week was like enlisted boot camp in that there was a lot of yelling, intense scrutiny, and mind games.

There were also females among us who stayed on the same corridor (passageway) but who had a separate bathroom (head). It was weird and understandable that nautical (navy) terms were used instead of civilian words (where we could get away with it). Right and left became starboard and port. The wall was the bulkhead. The floor was the deck. I was used to this because of my prior service, but a great deal of my colleagues was a little confused. Others had family that were navy or were prior enlisted like myself.

There was still an emphasis on teamwork, but now it was the thought process that was emphasized—your critical thinking, character, and attention to detail. When we got through with our training, we would be the ones giving the orders, so communication was key as well as your voice quality (i.e., a command voice). Imagine being in a stressful situation and the officer had a weak voice, or a weak character, or was unsure of themselves. Would you want to follow that person? That moment of hesitancy could cost lives in the extreme or material damage in another scenario.

Marching was emphasized to give each individual that experience of being in control of a group or leader—like it or not. Your bearing/presence was important. You had to at least project the perception that you could lead.

The analytical classes were there to get you to use critical thinking—to reason where you had to go to find the right answer and execute a plan, like celestial navigation or utilizing the supply system from the initial damage to receiving the part. You were also taught to know about your personnel you would be managing. You also had to be familiar with the UCMJ (Uniform Code of Military Justice).

There was also navigation and the engineering plant (and its operation) we had to have some knowledge of. It was like trying to sip from a fire hose. Exercise was just as important, and we PT'd (physically trained) as a group in the early morning—at four thirty or five o'clock—before showers, chow, and class. There was the day-to-day routine of boot camp, but there was an emphasis on critical thinking and responding to data presented to you—the ability to process then come up with a solution. This would come to a total of sixteen long weeks.

After the classes and marching throughout the week, we had a marching competition on Fridays and athletic activities on Saturday mornings, after which our weekend was ours until Sunday night unless we had duty, mandatory study hours, or a disciplinary situation we had to deal with. The weekends were, for the most part, our own.

As the weeks passed, the curriculum became increasingly difficult for me academically. I was thinking, *Not again.* So many people were behind me; I could not fail. I went to the extra classes. I stayed in on weekends, lost sleep, and dragged myself through classes and marches during the day. It was touch and go all the way, even until the very last exam where it came down to a decision by the director of the program. I can say I have never put a ship in peril or had any navigational incidents.

The ordeal was worth it. I believe at the time, a little more than 3 percent of the officers were African American. I finally made it, but could I keep it? So many times I was on the edge. So many times I did not think I would make it. All kinds of people were behind me, from my colleagues, senior enlisted officers, as well as other officers. Above and beyond this group, I would also have to thank God. I passed. I really passed. This phase was over—now it was SWOS (Surface Warfare Officer School).

Having had such academic problems in the past, I was determined not to have any distractions. I visited my family briefly between graduating OCS and my start of SWOS. My family had three members by then. My son Brian was born while I was at OCS on November 17, but I was unable to make it until Thanksgiving.

I had almost all my money going home (as I should have). I had a shoestring budget for ramen noodles and necessary hygiene products and uniform maintenance. Cynthia had the roughest time having to pay our bills and take care of our two children on such a small budget, in addition to me defaulting on a loan I took out so that my mom could have heart surgery. My biggest ally next to God was Cynthia.

I felt very focused going through SWOS. I felt like a monk. I hated the isolation, but it was paying off for me academically. I actually scored a perfect score on a module dealing with weapons, both foreign and our own. I also did well on a complicated materials, maintenance, and management (3M) course involving using a number of resources in tandem to get your final answer. We had a navigational practical where we actually would take turns driving, maneuvering, and giving orders, then rotating through to plot on the navigational charts. The sea was kind to us. I think only one person got a little seasick.

We practiced the navigational rules of the road. We had three ships out at this time, so we were able to simulate some maneuvers we would later use onboard our own ships. I felt like I might be picking this stuff up (finally). We passed our practical. I passed my written exams with no problems. There was one final school to go to before I would go to my ship, one more obstacle to leap over before I could go home. Cynthia was pregnant with our third child, Brandon, who would be due in September, the same time I would be reporting to the ship the USS *Thorn* DD-988—a gas-turbine-powered destroyer.

It was Gas Turbine Engineering Officer School I would be attending. We jumped right into the materials. We first went on a field trip to Boston to ride a gas turbine ship down to Newport, Rhode Island. Normally, we got this trip post-schooling, but scheduling had it this way. We learned the operations of the plant from a mechanical viewpoint in the engine room, then we went to where the EOOW (engineering officer of the watch) was to get a feel of what buttons we pressed had what effect in the engine room. This ride gave us an understanding of the ways what happens in the engine room/and engineering affects the ship as a whole.

Knowing what I do about Nidra—my great-great-great-grandmother who came to this country on a slave ship—how ironic that her great-great-great-grandson would be giving orders to white sailors to operate a ship that would also cross the Atlantic, not just to Africa but to Europe and Asia. I was deeply humbled and appreciative to Nidra, who made the journey as a child in bondage below the decks of a slave vessel.

It was so weird to be in a military which was predominantly Republican and holding moderate Democratic views like I did. I often felt conflicted at times in conversation, but I held my own, considering I was the only African American officer onboard (at this time). Although we rarely if ever talked about politics, we viewed our jobs as just that—without partisanship, regardless of who was in the White House. During my tenure in the military (both enlisted and officer), it was mostly Republican. It was Reagan through my enlisted years and Bush Sr. through my officer years, with Dick Cheney as secretary of defense. I left the military in February of 1993, just after Bill Clinton became president.

Having passed the tests and practical of gas turbine engineering, I would go to my ship, the USS *Thorn* DD-988, a destroyer. I would often joke with my officer colleagues as being "a fish out of water" since previously I was on submarines. It was such an irony that I would be back in Charleston, South Carolina as an officer. I really wanted to prove myself. Only I knew the hard work it took to get to this point. I wanted to qualify as soon as possible.

I visited home briefly before I reported to my ship. I believe I actually reported on my birthday—September 4. When I was at home, Cynthia was in full bloom of pregnancy with our third child, Brandon. This was 1990. Brandon would be born on September 21. The XO (executive officer) was also a family man with four children, so he understood. He allowed me to make a brief visit home. I got there (the hospital) a day after Brandon was born. Since the ship was in repair, getting state-of-the-art equipment as well as improvements to the weapons systems (the area I would be responsible for), I had time to take care of personal matters (like my son's birth). I saw my extended family for a few days. At this time, we lived in a Chicago suburb with Cynthia's sister and her daughter.

After catching up with family for a few days, it was back to the ship to qualify as much as I could while in port. It was also at this time that I was able to take other junior officer classes while the ship was being repaired. I was becoming familiar with my men and the equipment in my division. I was the Fire Control Officer (I was in charge of a variety of advanced weapons and missiles). I was also the Morale, Welfare and Recreation Officer.

The FCO (fire control officer) was a very highly-coveted position onboard—and I had it. My enlisted men were some of the brightest, well-mannered military men on board. My first division was all white, a great number of them from the South. I could not detect any attitude on their part. To the best of my knowledge, they were always professional in appearance and action. Even when some of them had some personal problems, when they showed up, they were ready. Having such a squared away (great) group of sailors gave me more time to work on my qualifications, which I did. At this time, I was the only black officer, and I did not feel I had any problems (racially) with my colleagues. We had differences of opinion (as men do), but we handled everything professionally, using the proper chain of command for any disputes.

After all the repairs and upgrades, it was time for sea trials. This is where we would test the ship for speed, maneuverability, readiness for sea, etc. There was a certain freedom being out on the open sea that is hard to describe. It was a great time to learn, experiment and to do. Going to sea after being in repairs was a great experience for a young junior officer—although I was not so young, my peers were in their early to mid-twenties. I was in my late twenties. I enjoyed the experience just the same. It was definitely a different feeling being above the water from being below it—the maneuverability yet vulnerability to the weather when you are on the seas, as opposed to going deep when you are on the submarine.

We were fortunate to have had some joint operations with the coast guard looking for drug traffickers. This coincided with some great liberty ports in the Caribbean like the Bahamas, the Virgin Islands, Jamaica, and Puerto Rico. Long before Guantanamo Bay was used to house the detainees, I remember going there for chemical, biological, and nuclear training. I also remember many damage control exercises. The scenery around Guantanamo was beautiful; we just could not go off base. I remember how clean and touristy Bermuda was. After all our various tests and trials and being confirmed ready for sea, we received our orders. I have never been on a surface ship for such a great length of time.

I was excited about going to the North Atlantic in November for a huge NATO exercise involving all our Northern European allies. As we got further and further north, the sea state was definitely rockier. As long as we were rocking side-to-side (port-starboard), it wasn't too bad. It was very disruptive front to back (fore and aft). The ship was a poor surfboard. The name of the exercise was called Operation Dragon Hammer—what a cool Nordic name.

There were various exercises and shipboard drills. The focus was on honing our skills and working as an international team together, not trying to dominate but to teach and to learn from all our allies. There was of course some showmanship, but nothing which compromised the mission or safety to personnel. It was quite a learning experience, especially for a junior officer wanting to qualify.

We traveled as far north as the Arctic Circle. There was this special navy ceremony I participated in called The Blue Nose. It was fun yet secretive, very fraternal. We went in and out of different fjords in Norway. We were supposed to have liberty in Stavanger, Norway, but there was a change to Amsterdam. I remember being a junior officer pulling into Amsterdam in the wee hours of the morning. It was still dark. There were so many contacts around us (other vessels large and small). I definitely depended heavily on my great navigation/operations team that led us in without a hitch.

I remember being with these guys when we were traveling in battle group formation and turning together and moving in sync. Now I realize how something as mundane as marching in time could prepare you to move in time/sequence with other ships. Timing and coordination/communication were so important—the difference between success and tragedy. The simple attention to details at both boot camps seemed to come together for an aha moment. I must say this was the pinnacle of my naval career. I was an officer giving orders on the bridge of a destroyer in formation that was part of a battle group during NATO exercises. It would not get any better than this. I felt like I was on a floating chessboard and we (my destroyer) were one of the highly valued bishops or knights protecting the king (aircraft carrier).

After pulling into Amsterdam and seeing the sites both culturally and otherwise, we were invited to tour the Heineken Brewery. The Dutch were very hospitable and gracious as well as professional. Being the morale, welfare, and recreation officer, I made sure I remembered how to thank them in their language ("Dank u wel"). The Dutch were impressed.

After finishing our NATO operations and leaving Amsterdam, we headed further south to Portsmouth, England, then further south rounding the Iberian Peninsula, entering the Mediterranean Sea. One of the most breathtaking sites is to be close enough to see the Rock of Gibraltar, having Spain (Europe) on one side and Morocco (Africa) on the other, to literally travel between two continents and see them so close together physically and worlds apart culturally. I felt on top of the world. During the NATO exercises, all my weapons worked properly. Now we were headed to Spain (one of its Balearic Islands called Ibiza). It was very scenic as well as historic. Several weeks later, we would have operations with our Mediterranean allies.

We spent Christmas through New Year's Day in Nice, France. What a holiday! The narrow, cobblestone streets, the beach, the cafés—I felt none of the animosity that people speak of the French. I found everyone to be friendly and hospitable. We even had dinner with one of our French liaisons out on the town—her treat. The food was unbelievably fresh, as if it were picked that day. The food was so colorful it could have been used for a photo shoot of fine French cuisine.

After the holidays, it was onward and eastward to Sicily, where we would not only refuel but order Sicilian pizza (for the whole ship). The pizza was so simple yet so good; it was a great crust. I realized what people meant when they say "Italian pizza is about the crust." The toppings were simple but complemented the crust.

After refueling and eating our pizza, we stayed for a day, then it was further eastward to Greece—more specifically, Athens. We were going to have some operations with our Mediterranean allies. I remember going on a tour which included Athens. Looking at the Acropolis and the Parthenon was fascinating, considering how long it had been standing. Another fascinating thing was how great the food was. I was also able to get some great souvenirs. When the ship got some repair work done in Souda Bay in Crete, the line to the local gyro place was outside and around the block. I had the best gyros ever.

After the repairs, we were off again. The next stop was Antalya, Turkey. We would have some operations along the way. I ate some great lamb in Antalya, Turkey. I also bought a beautiful meerschaum pipe. Its material is also known as sepiolite, a soft white mineral often used to make a smoking pipe. The figure on the pipe was a lion whose mane would change color over time with usage. I did not get a chance to see the transformation. I only smoked a few times, so the color did not change from the off-white color to the rich mahogany-like color it would have become. Smoking just wasn't my thing. Besides, too many of my relatives have died of various types of cancer. I just kept the pipe as a souvenir.

From Turkey we went to Haifa, Israel to engage in a few operations with the IDF (Israeli Defense Force). During one of the operations, I was part of a personnel transfer between ships. This gave me a chance to observe the Israelis at sea. These seemed like a dedicated group of young men wanting to complete the duty to their country. After the mission and a debriefing, we were able to tour Jerusalem. This involved a bus ride from Haifa through Tel-Aviv, then finally to Jerusalem. We were also able to visit the Dead Sea. If you are a spiritual person, you could understand why I had such an eerie feeling walking along some of the same places Christ walked, as well as visiting the Wailing Wall and seeing the Dome of the Rock. It is quite understandable why this place is so highly revered by so many people (and fought over just as much). I had such a solemn feeling at the Garden of Gethsemane. This was the place where Jesus asked to be spared, yet "God's will be done." And it was.

Many areas looked as if there were no changes in over two thousand years. It was very surreal to see the bands of Israeli soldiers walking around with Uzis amidst the crowds. To witness the various pilgrims from all around the globe at various shrines and historical places was truly fascinating and humbling. I had never seen such a reverence for the past. I was (and still am) in awe of Jerusalem. At this point, I have travelled to two continents, and soon would be entering my third.

We also visited Cyprus and Northern Cyprus. We ported in Limassol. The seaside was beautiful, and the Greeks have this dish similar to lasagna called moussaka that uses eggplant (or other vegetables) instead of pasta. Cyprus is divided into a Greek (southern) side and a Turkish (northern) side. The border was at the city of Nicosia. We actually had a small visit at the American Embassy there (as well as changed busses). North Cyprus gave me the impression of being older and more historic. We enjoyed ourselves in both places. I remember visiting some castle/monastery several hundreds of years old. Our cruise up to this point had been very routine, but that would soon change.

Our CO (commanding officer) received notification that our ship was to head to the Persian Gulf. Our ship had certain intelligence capabilities, making it useful to our operations there. I was now electrical officer. My division was more diverse. There was a "change of command" ceremony in Egypt.

When my feet touched Egypt, I was back home (several hundred years later) but in Northeastern Africa. It felt great to touch my third continent. There was time spent on the Red Sea refining ship handling skills of junior officers (such as myself) before entering the Persian Gulf. I remember rounding the Arabian Peninsula heading into my third ocean—the Indian Ocean. I took in the vastness of it all, the adventure of going to the Persian Gulf.

I did not know what to make of this Saddam Hussein (other than what I heard on the news). We were now part of a war effort against Hussein, so it was off into the Gulf we went. I remember the hours at battle stations" the mood was tense and edgy. We also had a helo (helicopter) detachment on board. We had them ever since our NATO operation months ago. These professionals flew missions and transported personnel/equipment. The war did not last long, and we were soon on our way again, having fulfilled our mission.

Before the helo detachment left our ship, there was time and fuel for some helo rides for volunteers. I had never been in a helo before so why not? Besides, I was glad the war was over, and there was a celebratory feeling onboard for a while. I felt a great feeling of freedom hovering then gliding across the open ocean with no land in sight. I was truly humbled at the ocean's vastness.

I was praying to God for a good outcome, which meant being able to head to loved ones. All the struggles I had before this point only seemed to validate this moment. I deserved to be here, yet I could not wait to be home. I believe we were away for nine months, but who's counting? I knew we were on our way home.

I remember porting in Jeddah, Saudi Arabia and visiting American contractors living in Saudi Arabia. This community of Americans invited the ship over for a barbecue. It was fantastic. I did not realize civilians so far from home could be so patriotic and appreciative at the same time. Their graciousness and hospitality was truly humbling—regardless of what you looked like, you were welcome. The contractors lived on these government-provided compounds. They looked and felt like gated communities in the States. It felt great to have a beer and some barbecue grilled American-style. Our hosts also took us out on the town in Jeddah. We visited various shops/bazaars. Gold was very reasonable here, as reasonable as diamonds were in Haifa, Israel. The smells of the spicy dishes tugged at my nose. There were other aromas combining to make this sensory kaleidoscope almost overwhelming but enjoyable.

We retraced a few ports, but for the most part it was a beeline home. Heading west past the Rock of Gibraltar with Africa visually prominent, I said a silent goodbye to the home of my black ancestors. Turning my head to starboard (right) I saw Europe, home of my white ancestors. Now I was leaving the Mediterranean Sea, home of three continents, three different groups of people (at least), and three major religions (at least). I will not forget. I have gone to three out of seven continents and three out of seven oceans—I was on my way home. There was a sense of satisfaction and accomplishment amongst the crew, as if we were a part of something. Although the war was brief and we had no casualties onboard, we still did go into harm's way and return safely. My remaining months on board were uneventful in comparison.

Getting home was a pleasure beyond words. To see my wife, my mother, my aunt, my grandmother, and my children made me appreciate God, my life, and life in general even more. I promised God when I was in the Gulf that if I returned safely, I would involve myself in something positive and life-affirming, something which celebrates life, embracing all peoples—I just had to find out what it would be.

We had various operations and some joint operations with Marines and SEALs, yet I could feel my time in the military slowly wind down. There was a new president (Clinton) in office, and it was going to be a different military. There was a reduction in forces, which I understood (and would soon be a part of). What was I going to do? My projected release would be late February 1993. I spent nine-and-a-half years in the military—where do I/we go from here? Then, I thought about my prayer to help others after leaving the Persian Gulf.

Chapter Seven

Fortunately, Cynthia was very supportive of whatever I had in mind. I would receive a stipend. I figure we could make it one year (with savings) until I retrained in something. Based on my experience and education, I could have had a higher paying job, especially with three kids and a wife, but I had to follow the voice. I wanted to do something life-affirming and fun. I wanted to do something to promote health, start out small and (possibly) work my way toward the medical field that I had walked away from years before. I thought of different occupations where I could work on my skills holistically yet have a foundation for further expansion if I chose to do so. I thought massage therapy.

I remembered a particular event I witnessed when I was enlisted. I saw a sailor (who was a former massage therapist) get rid of another sailor's migraine headache by applying pressure to certain areas of the neck and base of the skull. I was fascinated, but I was also studying oxygen generators at the time, and my priorities were military and family, but I did put the idea in my mind. Now it was time to bring it out. My life had reached a turning point. I was thirty. I was leaving the military, I had a new strategy. Now I needed a new place to stay.

The time was early 1993 and Seattle, Washington (as well as the Northwest in general) was the place to be. Although Mom wanted/expected me to come back to Illinois, Cynthia and I had other plans for our family. We thought opportunities in housing and education for ourselves and the children would be better in Seattle. The military would relocate us anywhere we wanted in the continental United States—for free. That was a godsend. A family accumulates a lot of stuff over a few years. This would be one less expense we would have to worry about. I had some time on the books. Cynthia and I packed the kids up and went via car, cross-country to Seattle—from Charleston, South Carolina to Seattle, Washington. What a drive.

We picked a great area (at the time). Renton, Washington, a suburb just southeast of Seattle, seemed a good fit for us. We picked a group of apartments that was close to a nationally-recognized elementary school and a shopping center. I deposited my stipend. I registered for my massage classes in Seattle. I could not wait to get started, to put my energies into a new project. Cynthia found a job at KinderCare, which was very convenient because the kids would be dropped off and fed and cared for.

I did not take a job at first so I could focus on my studies. I am so glad that I had gotten a stipend. I was getting straight A's in all my classes from anatomy and physiology to kinesiology and massage techniques. I volunteered to go on various projects, whether it was a bike race or a half-marathon or a civic event for AIDS or fibromyalgia. I welcomed it all because it was exposure and experience.

About seven or eight months into the year-long program, we could feel the economic pinch. I knew I had to do something, so what could I learn easily which could generate income and help with the bills and not interfere with my studies? I decided on being a certified nursing assistant (CNA). I would get used to dealing with people in a clinical setting and get used to taking vitals which could help me later. It was hard work, but it made me study even harder because I did not want to do this work. It was not the work I disliked. It was the volume of people I would have to get up. Being on the night shift, we were often short of people. I never felt like I had adequate time to treat these people with the dignity they deserved. This saddened me. I knew that if I were in their position (i.e., a patient who suffered from stroke, Alzheimer's, Parkinson's, or some other disease), I would want to look my best. I tried to be positive for the next few weeks while I scoured the papers to find a different job. It only took me a few weeks (thank God).

I was able to secure an interview with a security firm that had a contract with a computer firm in Bellevue, a Seattle suburb. I was fortunate because I had a degree as well as some familiarity with computers. It also helped that my interviewer was former military. I happened to be what they were looking for, and the job fit into my schedule (i.e., I worked nights so I could study/go to school during the day). Throughout this time, my grades did not slip, and I was maintaining a 4.0 average.

In the fall of our first year in Seattle, I would receive two heavy blows. One, my uncle Wilbert died. He was a great inspiration, the only man in our family who had earned/received a doctorate. He was one of the reasons I played tennis. He was pivotal in my changing my major to psychology at the U of I. When I attended the University of Illinois, its psychology department was rated rather high (I believe in the top ten). Uncle Wilbert was like a second father to me. He used to take me to the Chicago State University Cougars basketball games. What a great time we would have. He and Aunt Mentha had no children of their own, so us nephews and nieces received a great deal of attention and mentoring.

He was also instrumental in getting me, my older siblings, and my cousins into the National Summer Youth Sports Program (NSYSP) for a few summers. From the early mornings to the afternoons, we learned to swim, play football, basketball, tennis, volleyball, wrestle, and run track. The program gave us a safe place to go to during the summer. It was located on the campus of Chicago State University at Ninety-Fifth and Dr. Martin Luther King Drive. We got lunch and a snack at the end of the day. We also met other kids on the south side. It was a perfect program for inner city youth.

This torrent of memories hit me when I received the notification of his death from Aunt Mentha. She said it so plainly over the phone, yet Aunt Mentha was unflappable. I don't ever remember her not being in control of a situation or herself. This is not saying she would not let you know (without a doubt) if you crossed the line; she just had a certain composure about her.

I had to get airline tickets for myself only. We could not afford more. Aunt Mentha and Uncle Wilbert had retired to Covington, Tennessee— although in his case I must say semi-retired because he taught at a community college in a city north of Covington. He also still enjoyed senior-level competitive tennis. He had created such a passion for the sport in Covington that after his passing, the city established the Wilbert Jackson Open Invitational Tennis Tournament. He definitely would have been pleased. He and Aunt Mentha were featured in the November 1991 issue of **Ebony** magazine in an article about seniors in retirement. I have a couple of old newspaper clippings of Aunt Mentha presenting the winners with the trophy.

This great man, who was also a WWII veteran, also did the lion's share of the family research for the 1992 family book. I asked Aunt Hertha and Aunt Mentha about certain events. I also received my copy of the book as well as what happened at the family reunions in years past. To hear/read about the story of Nidra and family ignited my curiosity to know more about this slave girl and her grandson (my great-grandfather, Charles Henry). When I was in Tennessee, I kept my eyes open and asked questions of relatives. I actually saw Bethel Street. I began to realize (when I was more than thirty years old) the gravity of being a Bethel in Covington.

Uncle Wilbert had such an impact on Covington. This was reflected by those in attendance at the funeral. There were black, white, old, young, rich, poor, powerful, and everyday people, just the way my uncle would have wanted it. Uncle Wilbert just had one of those personalities of transcendence. He could (and did) talk to anyone. He listened and actually cared about what you thought, so I guess he found his calling in the field of psychology. It was perfect for him. Being a black male made it even more significant since so many of us (black males) keep how we are feeling to ourselves. There was a certain sense of hopelessness or "why bother, no one cares," but Uncle Wilbert cared, and many black youth opened up to him. No matter what state of mind you were in when you first began talking to him, you were better by the end of the conversation. More importantly, you were energized to do something about your situation. He would be a major influence in me earning my doctorate in the field of naprapathy (which specializes in disorders of the connective tissue [muscle, ligament and bone] and the treatment of these disorders through the use of manual adjustment, nutrition, modalities, and therapeutic exercise).

I was in a fog prior to going to Tennessee—my wife Cynthia and I were going through our own rough times in our relationship. My uncle's death (ironically) helped me renew my commitment to the relationship upon my return to Seattle.

It seemed like it was a week or two later when my Aunt Jewel died. She was my uncle Thomas's wife. Uncle Thomas was Aunt Mentha's older brother and younger brother to my deceased grandfather Samuel. This couple had been married for over forty years. They were the epitome of a black middle-class/professional couple. They both taught years before in the Covington school district. Both attended historically black colleges. Both had been in the Black Greek System (she was Alpha Kappa Alpha he was Kappa Alpha Psi). He was once named Kappa man of the year for the City of Memphis, Tennessee—a great honor.

Now my uncle's "alpha sweetheart" was gone. When they were together, you could actually feel the love they had for each other, the love born out of a common struggle and perseverance. I am sure they had their struggles like any other couple, but I am sure there were more good days than bad. Aunt Jewel and Uncle Thomas, as well as Aunt Mentha and Uncle Wilbert, were role models for the rest of us in the family—educated, prosperous, and involved in the community. It was possible to learn just being in their presence and listening to their conversations. They held so much knowledge about the past and how we as a people combated the adversity. Now all the senior Bethels—Uncle Thomas, Aunt Hertha and Aunt Mentha—were single.

I went back to Seattle with a renewed interest in making the relationship work. I was so focused on work and school that my family was being neglected. I have always been somewhat of a workaholic (to be honest, very much a workaholic). It's just that other family members had been so successful. I was wondering, would I ever make my mark? Would I ever take my place with the other Bethel's?

Christmas was rather sparse due to funds, but Cynthia always made sure we had a great meal and a festive time, and the kids were just happy it was Christmas (and we were together). The house was decorated beautifully on our limited budget. A year in Seattle was coming to an end. What a year—academic success, financial/family struggle, and death—yet I was getting nearer to my goal (graduation). The program would be over in a few months, and then I would begin my job search.

It was January 1994, ten years from when I first met Cynthia in Chicago while I was at Great Lakes Naval Base. By then, we were in a three-bedroom apartment with three children in a suburb of Seattle. The kids were in a good school. I was working, and Cynthia was, too. School for me would be done in a month or two. The future looked so bright—or so it seemed.

I had no idea what a gender bias there was in the field of massage therapy (against males). I understood the difficulty women experience in certain professions. I also did not realize being a black male also had its unique problems (even in Seattle). I remember calling one place and having them say they could really use a male on staff (since they had none). This place was in West Seattle. I felt very positive about this place. We exchanged a firm handshake and had direct eye contact. I was assertive and not aggressive. The owner did let me massage her and said it was good, but somehow she was not as enthusiastic about me as she was over the phone (when she could not see me). I did not have any real proof, only the look of slight surprise and an immediate correction (as if I did not see the first response) that you get when you are a black male. Massage is so subjective—who's to say if I could have been successful there if the clientele had the same attitude as the owner?

Graduation day came. I graduated at the top of my class—the only African American, the most volunteer hours, yet no job offers. Bills needed to be paid. I attempted a partnership with a white, female classmate of mine who I got along well with. The things we tried did not work. In my frustration, I began just visiting every chiropractor in Renton, Washington (near my house). The first chiropractor I visited was female, and she was very honest. She had a bad experience of her massage therapist trying to steal her patients, so she stopped having massage therapists altogether. The second chiropractor I visited was Dr. Clark. He was a very successful chiropractor on the corner of two major streets in Renton. I met his office manager Robin and handed her my résumé. She took my résumé and said that the doctor was busy. Before I got into my car, Dr. Clark came out the door of the office and welcomed me back in. The rest was history.

To date I have worked with a total of six chiropractors—four males and two females—in my twenty years of practice. Dr. Clark and I worked well together. I decreased the muscular tension in the spine (or other target area). This enabled Dr. Clark to get an easier adjustment. The adjustments seemed to last longer with the massage therapy (my patients told me this). I also had regular clients just for massage. I was now working two jobs: the security job at night and working with the chiropractor during the day. My income did increase. At this time, my goal was to help people, and at the same time I was improving my techniques. I did not need my own business now. I really just wanted to focus on building my skills and people spreading the word.

Things seemed to be getting better between Cynthia and me. The kids were thriving in school and making friends. I was sad I could not send money home to my mother and brother in Illinois. My brother Ted had multiple sclerosis at this time. Mom said she needed the money to help with the bills. I could feel the desperation in her voice, yet I had my family in Seattle I was supporting. I was torn. Although I was not poor, I was not confident enough financially to send money. This ate at me bit by bit (although I discussed it with no one). I felt I had to be successful here. I did not want my children's education to decrease (which is what would have happened at one of the rural schools back home). I did not have the funds for private school back home. My kids had to stay here to have a future. I also did not like the race relations/segregation that seemed to be in our area of Illinois. I am sure Mom thought I would move back to Illinois after I got out of the military. I thought I could do better and the children would have a better future in Seattle.

I remember a story I overheard as a child about my grandfather (my mom's dad) Odis Wooley visiting Seattle when he was a young man. He was impressed (especially at that time) with the lack of threat and of freedom of movement which he did not experience in rural Arkansas or the City of Chicago. Both of those areas were segregated at the time, so the thought of moving to Seattle post-military was a nice fresh start for me and my family. I wanted my children to go to school experiencing the diversity I had (at least from kindergarten to second grade).

My work at the chiropractor's office was increasing. People were asking for me by name. We also had an influx of Russian and Eastern European clients due to the fact the Berlin Wall had been destroyed and Seattle was a port of entry. There was an odd mix of people due to political situations. Although we did not have any Somali or East African patients, a number of them had come to the area due to the political upheavals in their countries. The suburb was becoming increasingly diverse. I even learned a few words in Russian to greet the patients as well as direct them on my massage table (e.g., right side, left side, on your stomach, on your back). A patient called Nadia gave me some elementary Russian books and helped me through the alphabet, which was a challenge for me. Today I remember very little. What a shame. She was originally from Belarus.

Life seemed to be filled with work, and I had to balance between work and family. I was on top of the world, then the phone call came. My grandmother Bernice (my mom's mom) died. What a blow. We thought her lung cancer had gone into remission, but it came back with a vengeance. She was in her seventies. She had struggled with hypertension for as long as I could remember. Many of her seven children smoked (my mom included). My grandfather smoked camel cigarettes. My grandma never smoked (she was the only one in the family to get lung cancer). I regretted not having the funds to go to her funeral. Cynthia made the suggestion of me going to my employer and asking for an advance, but I did not feel right doing that. I knew there would be an issue with certain family members since I attended the funerals in my father's side last year. I simply did not have the money to spare.

My mom understood. She had the monumental task of taking care of my brother who was living with multiple sclerosis. My brother was very independent. Although he was in a wheelchair at this time, he had such great upper body strength he hardly needed any assistance at all. My brother was even stronger internally. Here he was ten years my junior at twenty-two and dealing with such tough life issues. I admired him so much.

Mom had been a truck driver (18wheeler) for a few years. She and her partner Hosea had travelled cross-country a few times. I believe they went through every state within the Continental United States. I guess I get my love for and curiosity of travel through her. As my brother's condition progressed and different treatments were tried, it became apparent that she would have to come off the road and get a local job. She did, without hesitation or remorse. Mom was all about family and sacrifice (if need be).

My brother's doctor and rehab team were at Rush Hospital in Chicago. He seemed to like the team of doctors and rehab personnel that were working with him. He had to maintain his strength. Mom would take him to his appointments and juggle her work as well. I felt so low, so guilty. I did not send money, but I had my own family to support.

Grandma's funeral came and went and was well-attended by family, friends, and other acquaintances. I got the full story when I talked to my brother. He and my mom seemed closer now. It is a strange thing about tragedies in a family—they seem to either bring you closer or tear you apart. Mom and Dad were definitely people that got stronger with adversity. My brother, who had his difficulties with Mom following the death of our father, seemed to be a different, more mellow person now. My mom was definitely his advocate for treatment, services, and rehab. I did have my own family and problems, but it seemed small in comparison to what my mother and brother were dealing with.

Cynthia and I seemed to be getting closer together; there seemed to be more balance in our relationship. The kids were growing, enjoying school, and making new friends. My daughter was in a Christmas play which also featured the celebration of Kwanzaa (which begins the day after Christmas). This was the first play I had seen any of my children in. It felt so good to see Brianna on stage and to walk hand-in-hand with her after her performance, her little smile beaming Christmas cheer.

My daughter that past summer had invited three of her friends over for a birthday sleepover. The girls were white—there was no drama from the parents. The boys had an outing at my wife's friend's house. The girls had a great time. We went to IHOP the next morning for pancakes.

This was my world for the early to mid-1990s. I had a nagging feeling things were going to change. I had these vague dreams about my brother Ted. I also had these vague dreams of myself doing something which was not chiropractic but not massage either, which had an element of adjustment/manipulation but also stretching and traction. I wondered about what these things meant, but I did not tell my dreams to anyone because it seemed too weird. I didn't even understand them, so I definitely knew other people would not understand.

It was August 1995, our tenth wedding anniversary. We were closer. The children were eight (Brianna), almost seven (Brian), and almost five (Brandon). I surprised Cynthia with another (better) wedding ring a few weeks before our actual ten-year anniversary. She was so happy to receive the ring. We were a happy family. Brandon's fifth birthday came with great celebration. Brian's seventh birthday came in November also with great celebration.

Then it was Christmas time—the best Christmas ever for our little family. Cynthia and I had gone shopping for the kids. I spent much more than I had planned, but I felt like just as big a kid as my children, which Cynthia mentioned to me. Christmas came, and the gifts and toys were unwrapped. The children played, and we joyfully watched. The meal was magnificent (as always). I had more purchasing power with my two jobs and Cynthia with her job at KinderCare. I felt so happy. I felt like this was what middle class was like. I felt like a husband/provider/father—I felt important.

One phone call the next day changed all that. I am still in a daze thinking about it almost twenty years later. The phone call came while I was at the computer security job on the night shift, the same job I had won two plaques and commendations at. The first award came for taking emergency action to prevent fire during a storm. The second award came for taking emergency action to prevent further damage of an electrical fire. I felt I was making some progress. I was not rich, but we were a family. We were stable, and we were together. Our kids were developing into fine little people.

Then the phone call came from my Aunt Phyllis. My mom had suffered a massive coronary before entering the Dan Ryan on an entry ramp. My cousin Paul, who lived with my mom now to help out around the house, was her passenger. She had just come from visiting my brother, who was at Rush Hospital receiving therapy for one of his relapses with multiple sclerosis. My cousin tried to revive/resuscitate my mom, but to no avail. She was taken to St. Bernard's hospital on the south side of Chicago. Sadly and ironically, my grandma Bernice (my mom's mom) died there a year or so ago. After getting relieved from my job, I went home and quickly packed. It was late at night. Cynthia and the kids took me to the airport. It would be the last time I would see them for a few years other than talks on the telephone and pictures sent through the mail. What a holiday season this was turning out to be. It was unforgettable (in the worst way).

Chapter Eight

My aunts picked me up from the airport to give me the lowdown of what was going on with my mother and brother. I was listening but I felt outside myself, as if I were a witness as well. I talked to various doctors about Mom's condition. She was in ICU. The prognosis was not good.

Mom said in the past if she were on life support, she would want it terminated. I wonder how many others have been in the situation I was in? Mom was on life support, and she would want to be terminated. I could not do it. I wasn't ready to make that decision—not yet. Being a Catholic (a very lapsed one), I struggled with this situation. Was my faith being tested, or was this a life issue I had to settle? I had discussions with relatives, back and forth for the next few days as bodily systems slowly shut down.

My cousin Paul and I would visit Rush Hospital in the morning to encourage my brother in his therapy. He was making great progress. We would visit Mom on life support in the afternoons/evenings, visiting my aunts in between. We went back and forth, but the decision was still mine to make.

My brother Ted wanted to see her and to give me his input. I was worried that seeing her with the tubes and other equipment attached would depress him, affecting his own therapy. But she was his mother, too. I had to let him see. We helped transfer him into the car. I was really worried about a relapse with his multiple sclerosis. He wheeled himself into her room and parked by her bedside. He held her unresponsive hand. He bowed his head and wept. I had never seen my brother cry as a man. He said it softly at first, then said more firmly, "Let her go."

"Let her go." It was settled. I knew what I had to do. We took my brother back to Rush from St. Bernard's. I informed my aunts what the decision was and asked them if there were any objections. I received none. They did not want me to cremate Mom, but this too was also in her wishes, according to my brother Ted. Before this point, I had prayed for a sign, something that would give me hope or reason to pause, but each major organ system was in failure. The EEG was a flat line.

It was time to let go. I had my answer. Right or wrong, a decision had to be made—one I have lived with to this very day. It was ironic how I became the holder of my mom's life, the woman who had gone through so much to have and raise me. And I decided to let her go home. Was I playing God? No, I just wanted her to be free and abide by her wishes.

The hospital staff said they would remove the equipment and let her go, and they gently suggested that I did not have to stay and watch. I said I wanted to stay—I had to. Maybe a miracle would occur; stranger things have happened. The equipment was removed, and I was allowed to stay in her room. I sat down, holding her hand until she had gone home. I felt sadness, grief, and relief all at the same time. I stayed for a while after life had passed from her, after all traces of any vital signs were apparent, and several minutes after that.

I went out to the nursing station and told them it was finished. In some of their eyes I saw tears. She had made an impact on them as well as the other people her life touched. I took care of the necessary paperwork and left the hospital that my grandmother—and now mother—had died in. I felt numb. I went to my aunt's house and talked with the gathered family members. Now began the process of planning for the memorial since mom chose cremation. I also had to plan getting the relatives in from out of town, etc. The service was held on January 8. What a way to begin 1996.

My mom wanted to be cremated and for the ashes to be placed in the gravesite of my father. At the memorial service, instead of having a preacher who did not know my mother preach, I had family members give their fondest memories of my mom. I got so much strength and reassurance from them. I listened to tales of her kindness and strength. I was strengthened by listening.

After the memorial service, we all went to the gravesite, and I placed the container of the ashes in the gravesite (not casket) of my father. This was my first time holding a living being's ashes. It was an eerie feeling, holding the remains of the woman that brought me into the world. I gave her back to the earth to be with my father.

The days that followed were very involved in terms of settling accounts, insurance, and assets. I could also now focus on the living—my brother in particular, as well as my own family. My brother could walk with a walker or canes for support. He was a real trooper at the hospital—always on time for his therapy, always maximizing his time and his effort. It probably reminded him of his football training in high school and his star running back status. He was twenty-three (almost twenty-four). He had contracted multiple sclerosis at twenty, but it was a very aggressive form of relapsing/remitting MS. It would come, hit hard, and go.

The treatments, therapy, and drugs helped to serve as a levy or buffer against the storm of MS. The drugs are much better now. Although I am not a big fan of drug usage, I could see the difference in mood and performance the drugs allowed. Some of the drugs had side effects, but I felt the benefits were greater. They at least helped him to deal with life and keep physically strong. My brother also grew marijuana for self-use, which I did not find out about until later. Being the older brother, I wish I could take this away. I wish he did not have to deal with this—but he did.

I was becoming more and more distant from my family in Seattle. My wife Cynthia was wondering when I would be back (as she should). I sent money from the insurance and dissolved CD, but that would be gone soon. The elephant in the room was asking the questions "When are you going back to your family?" and "Are there any relatives that I could trust here to take care of my brother?" The answer to both questions was a wobbly "I don't know." I could have left him with my cousin Paul, but my brother felt more comfortable with my presence, and I felt my brother was my responsibility, but I also had a responsibility to my wife and children.

My other siblings were over a thousand miles away and had their own lives. My aunts lived in or near Chicago roughly fifty miles away. My brother did not want to leave the home that the family had built. By coincidence, the house was accessible. All the doorways and halls were wide enough for his wheelchair. The house was a ranch-style home with a connected garage.

Another reason my brother did not want to leave Illinois was because an aunt did extensive research and legwork in finding out programs my brother was eligible for, and she was able to make it happen for him. If he moved out, he might not be as lucky, not to mention the transition time between state residency. I definitely did not have any bureaucratic or administrative connections. My aunt worked in this realm with the VA. She knew certain ins and outs, not only federally but how it pertained to Illinois residents and my brother's status. My family lived in a third floor walk-up with no elevator—no accessibility with my brother's wheelchair. Also, where would my brother stay if he moved in with us?

Our house in Illinois was a beautiful brick home, but due to its rural location and where it was located, it would not get much on the market. My employers were also running thin on patience. Everyone wanted answers, but I had none. Multiple sclerosis is not one of those diseases that follow a definite timeline. Each case is different, and how it attacks the nervous system of each individual is also different.

Cynthia wanted to move back to Illinois. Although she would not have liked living at that house, she would have made the sacrifice. I was thinking of the children—their education, futures, and options would have definitely been more limited than where they were now. I also knew that until I figured this thing out, I needed a source of income. At this time, you could look in the daily paper's "help wanted" section and find something. I figured I needed something that freed me up during the day so that I could take my brother to and from his various appointments as well as be there for him.

I found something. It was called a habilitation aide (later termed direct service professional). This sounded pretty ambiguous, but I decided to give it a shot. This place was on the north side of Chicago; a home for the developmentally disabled. I had a BS in psychology. I remember getting an A in childhood and development class. I figured it was worth a try. The biggest advantage was that I would be working nights, so this freed me during the days to help out at home. I took the test and was called back for an interview, and was offered the job. This was around March, three years post-military. How my life had changed.

I was in an orientation class with an eclectic group of human beings. There were college students who needed jobs. There were older individuals displaced by other jobs. There were people like me, just looking for a job to meet their circumstance. I figured with my background I would at least have the patience to deal with the residents. Some had cerebral palsy (CP). Some had Down's syndrome. Some had autism. Some had seizure disorders. Some had a variance of the aforementioned or their own unique disorder. I got along well with my classmates. There were at least thirty of us. We had a great rapport. (At least five of us are still here after eighteen years.)

There was a final written test after weeks of training and observation. After taking the exams and grading them, the teacher, who was very hands-on, asked us if we wanted to know who the highest score went to. I immediately answered no. The thirty others in the class wanted to know. The instructor was at a quandary—it was me.

After passing the class and going to work, I would take my brother to physical or occupational therapy sessions in the mornings. We would hang out and run errands until late afternoon. We would eat, and I would go to sleep until I had to get up later for work. The pattern continued for a few weeks. I would send money back home, but it was not enough. Cynthia needed an answer so she could make decisions regarding the children and herself. I was unable/unwilling to provide an answer.

I lost my jobs in Washington State because of lack of attendance. Cynthia was able to make arrangements with her brother in Southern California. She and the kids moved in with her brother and niece. I felt bad and irresponsible, but I knew where the children were in California would be better than where I was in Illinois. Cynthia moved on. We were already physically separated—now we were divorced. I felt like a jerk, a failure.

I thought about leaving Illinois, but I prayed. The prayer was, "If I was able to get into a new program of physical therapy assistant at Kaukakee Community College, I would stay. If not, I would go." (I had been unable to get into a program in Washington State, so I thought for sure I would be going back home.) I felt that by having an associate's degree as a physical therapy assistant, I could more competently help my brother with stretches and exercises at home.

To my surprise, I was able to get in. The first class last year was all white. Ours would be the second class. There was only one other African American in the program besides me. I thought I had been out of school too long, but my recent background as a massage therapist, as well as my past science background at the U of I, surely helped my cause.

I had been very impressed with the PTs and PTAs at Rush Hospital who were assisting my brother. I helped/assisted when I was able, and sometimes helped them when my brother was finished with his therapy.

I was hoping that by expanding my knowledge, I could help my brother at home. The degree was secondary.

When my brother was released from therapy (he had learned to drive with "sticks" while in therapy), he would drive to the community college and other places to be with his friends and run errands. I would stretch him out, and he would do his exercises with the PTs. This school process brought us closer together; in fact, I wanted him to go back, as long as it was not stressful to him.

The program was from 1996 to 1998. I took to anatomy and physiology easily earning an A in the first semester from one of the toughest instructors. I also had physics, which I also got an A in. The other classes I was in I also got A's in the first semester. I was on the president's list (those having a 4.0 average). It did not last. I got a B in my second semester of anatomy and physiology and a B in (of all things) English. I became engrossed in my books, trying to get all As again. I was still helping around the house, but not as much as initially. My ambition, as always, was eating at me.

The program lasted two years. The first year went great—my brother had found someone to share his life with, someone who was helping him as much if not more than me. I was juggling school, work, and my brother's medical appointments. I was sure I could do this. The program was intensifying. I was admitted to Phi Theta Kappa (ϕθκ), which is the two-year college's version of Phi Beta Kappa (ϕBK). I began working on my internships now, and my brother's girlfriend was helping him significantly. She had even moved in. In fact, by early 1998, my "little" brother would be a dad for the first time.

My first internship was at Christ Hospital in Oak Lawn, Illinois. I worked with some great PTs who were young, fun, focused, and most importantly, knowledgeable. Now was the time to put all the knowledge I had learned into practice. Therapy is beautiful, seeing people get better over time—seeing people move more freely, have a better gait (walking) pattern, increase in endurance, and do the things they wanted to do again. I felt blessed by having this opportunity to help the people. I made mistakes like any intern, but I was fortunate to have therapists who understood.

My next internship was at the Rehabilitation Institute of Chicago (RIC), the pinnacle of rehab in the region, if not the entire United States. Things were very fast-paced here. There were floors that had their own department (i.e., spinal cord injury, pediatrics/minors, etc.). The amount of information was intense, yet again, the therapists were very supportive. They were encouraging, but they never hesitated to make corrections if necessary. I would go there directly after working at my night job on the north side of Chicago. I either changed/washed up in the men's bathroom at RIC or changed in my car (as I had done at Christ Hospital).

The weeks flew by. I chose pediatrics, and I had a few patients to work with after my initial orientation. After working with children/minors here, I realized that was not the area for me. I got through my internship and enjoyed the amount of information and camaraderie we had as therapists from different fields working together (i.e., physical therapy, occupational therapy, and speech therapy). I enjoyed the teamwork we had and the occasional beers we would have on Friday nights, ending a great week in therapy.

My last internship was with Mercy Hospital in Chicago, near/in Bronzeville, which is a mixed-income, up-and-coming, historically African American neighborhood rich in history and tradition. It was my final internship. I had my own patient load (supervised, of course). I was also exposed to home health, long-term care, and nursing homes. There was a great variety of learning and environments to choose from. I still worked my forty hours at night and went to my internship Monday to Friday.

I enjoyed Mercy a great deal because of the diversity of the patients. Until this time, my patients were mostly of one demographic. Having grown up on the south side, I wanted to feel as if I had given something back to Chicago, especially to the south side. I worked on people from the south side—people from Bronzeville, Bridgeport, Chinatown, and Pilsen. In other words, these people represented the Chicago I knew and grew up with—the ethnic, grittier side of Chicago. These people had a lot of heart and personality, which in turn made me try harder. I pushed them maybe a little bit harder than the others. I was also a South Sider. I remember having used some of my Polish/Russian words, as well as Spanish (that I had four years of in high school). Regardless of color, these were my people—Chicagoans (South Siders). Don't get me wrong—in terms of exposure to techniques and information, RIC was the best, but Mercy Hospital was like going home.

This was a very active time for me. I would be an uncle by March 10, 1998. There was now a "little" Ted—the fourth generation of the name Theodore, first starting with my great-uncle, then my father, then my brother, and now his son. My brother was elated. Things had come full circle for him. Even with his multiple sclerosis, he was determined to be a great dad, better than myself. It was I who admired him for his family instincts and devotion.

This prompted me to apologize and ask forgiveness from Cynthia, which she accepted. I wanted to come back, but she had moved on. (I could not blame her.) How long was a person supposed to wait, especially when there were young children whose needs must be met? I still loved and admired her for her strength, stability, and just being the mother that she was. Motherhood always seemed to suit her, and everyone seemed to notice as well as comment on it. When it came to family, she was the rock.

The end of my internship came, it was a heartfelt goodbye. I received compliments from my therapists. We had a small, close-knit group which was quite diverse. My lead/senior therapist was a Japanese American lady. Her right arm was a Dutch therapist. And there was a very experienced African American young lady with a wealth of experience who helped me a lot. They were all female. I enjoyed their energy and sense of community/cooperation. On my last day in the clinic, the lead therapist and the two aforementioned ladies took me to a great restaurant in Chinatown that served sushi. I was hoping I might be offered a position, but it was not meant to be.

In a few weeks, graduation came, and I was offered a position at a state institution for the developmentally disabled in Kankakee, along the Kankakee River. My lead PT was Indian, a woman who was tough but fair. After graduation, there were some financial issues in paying off my final classes. Although I had secured a job, it was before I received my first check from my new job. I was in the process of paying bills and back taxes from when I was married. I also had wages going to child support (which I wholeheartedly agreed with). Unknown to me, money was taken out by the bank of a joint account. My brother and I had to pay the bills around the house. I could not explain the situation adequately to my brother, who thought I was trying to cheat him or mismanaged our funds. I had focused so intensely on finishing my classes and the program (I was the only African American in our program at this time) that I was juggling my expenses to get by. A rift occurred between my brother and me. I was asked to go, and I did. I knew his fiancé would take care of him. He also had a son now. This was all probably for the best, but I hated leaving on bad terms with my brother.

I thought since I was working two jobs now—one during the day, and another at night—the only time I needed lodging would be on my days off. I felt awkward at first. I had my possessions at the time (not much) in my Nissan Sentra. I was doing a lot of driving back and forth between my job in Chicago at night and my job during the day in Kankakee. I used the local Laundromat in Momence, Illinois.

I saved up quite a bit and asked Cynthia if I could visit the children for Christmas (it was 1998). Thankfully, she agreed. This would be the first time I would see the kids since my leaving in 1995—the day after Christmas. What irony. Cynthia and the children had moved into a place in Southern California called Lake Elsinore. When I visited, it was so beautiful—a fantastic place, especially for children. The children were bigger, and they had bigger questions. I muddled my way through it, wondering to myself if what I was saying was true or not. I loved these little people, yet I knew I had wronged them greatly. I brought presents. We went on shopping sprees, yet nothing could compare to what their mother had done for them. There was no catch-up after that day, so I decided to make the best of it.

Cynthia's brother was a truck driver, with a beautiful daughter named Becky. How fortunate my children were to have such an attentive and protective older cousin. The kids seemed happy and healthy. I wanted to come back so bad, especially at that time. No one knew of my living arrangements. I wanted neither pity nor I-told-you-sos. It was apparent Cynthia had moved on, and I was happy for her.

The kids and I went to Magic Mountain and Disneyland. We had a great time bonding, and it was over all too soon. I know in their minds there were so many unanswered questions, yet in my own mind there were unanswered questions about my purpose and where I fitted in. I thought about the past at this time, about the Bethel Family origins. As a family man, I felt like a failure. I felt no self-pity. I am who I am. The Lord has always been there for me, no matter how stupid the mistakes, and this was no exception.

As I kissed the kids and left, I knew I had to delve in deeper to who I really was if I were to maintain my sanity. After my holiday vacation with the kids, it was 1999. Three years after my mother passing on, my life turned inside out.

I had a very close friend at this time, and she knew of my living situation. She had at one time worked for the MS (multiple sclerosis) Society of Chicago. She was a big help with recommendations for my brother. We met at an MS meeting at RUSH hospital, that I felt was quite informative. She talked to a friend about my situation (unknown to me). He made the suggestion of the Y (YMCA). I thought about it and decided to ask about the prices. I happened to meet the criteria. At least now I did not feel like a nomad I had a place to put my stuff. I felt a little more stable and settled.

I did not visit my brother. He did not know where I was. In my mind, I wished him and his little family well. I would periodically just drive past the house—they never knew. I could see the house and the lawn were being maintained—why was I worrying? I had to focus my energy on something now that I had a place to stay.

I decided since it was 1999 (and I had listened to the *Left Behind* series on cassette while driving—I thought the end was near anyway) I would do something totally crazy. I would run in my first marathon at the age of thirty-seven. I figured if the world was going to end by 2000 (as many had thought), I would do most of the things I wanted to do that year. I had never run great distances before, but like massage therapy, I was intrigued by the idea.

Due to changes in Medicare and billing at this time, our PT had to let us go. I can't believe I lost my first job as a PTA. I still had my license as a massage therapist, so to get my skills together and do some community service, I volunteered for an organization that worked for people with AIDS. It helped build my rapport with clients. Since working with the disabled and people who are challenged in their communication skills, I was getting better at reading facial expressions and nonverbal cues. This knowledge helped immeasurably when working with people with AIDS. I was able to apply just enough pressure and decrease it when needed. I had a couple of shifts during the week.

There seemed to be a lot of PTA's in the job market at that time, so I thought, why not try massage therapy again? I applied to different places and I got a callback from a spa in Downtown Chicago. Ironically, it was on Chicago Street. There was this funky 1990s nouveau trendy look. I walked down into this cavernous salon/spa which was spacious and inviting and owned by African Americans. I would be lying if I did not say I had a great sense of pride working here. It was black-owned, and I had a rapport with the employees. Some were white, and there was one Korean lady who ran the nail department. It seemed like a great work environment. The split was 50/50. I was not mad at that considering I had not really worked for awhile (other than with my PT patients and my brother with MS). It seemed like a family atmosphere. This was around February or March. In my off time, I ran in my little room at the Y. (I did not want anyone to know I was running a marathon.)

Being at this spa made me reflect on my blackness. Where did I come from? Who was Nidra, Caroline, Charles Henry? What was Black? The family of the owners was a regular "black rainbow," from the father (richly dark), who was the head stylist, to his sons, who were middle tone in complexion. One son was a stylist, and the other managed operations. Their sister was fair-skinned, with a beautiful tightly-curled blonde afro. The mom was also fair-skinned with long, straight hair. The sister handled the natural styling (i.e., braids, twists, etc.) department, while her mother handled all the spa operations (i.e., massage, wraps, waxing, etc.) The family seemed very successful to me.

One receptionist was fair skinned; another was Polish. One of the natural stylists in training was Puerto Rican. We all worked in this multicultural/multiethnic group. The place was in a racially changing gentrifying community, and we had all types of people coming in—the old and the new. I enjoyed it because it was more diverse than any work environment I had worked in prior to this (other than the military and the U of I).

I was glad my hands were busy again. Massage therapy was my passion. It was great to see someone come in one way and leave totally relaxed, able to move their bodies more freely. We had a number of local celebrities come in: a basketball player from the Bulls, a news anchor lady, some pillars of the financial community. I had my share of performers in downtown dance/plays and spoken word performances. Two of my most famous clients at this time was Hinton Battle, the three-time Tony Award winning dancer/performer, and Bonnie DeShong, a famous local radio personality at the time. Both of these people came to me more than just once, so I thought of it as a great honor.

I felt inspired being around all the black people that were doing things. The feeling was electric. I thought of my life and wondered could it get any better. I did not have my own business, but was that what I really wanted? Not everyone is an entrepreneur, and there was no shame in that. I had to think realistically. With the child support and other bills I had, not to mention my credit rating, I simply did not have the cash on hand to start a business. This place was well-funded with an assortment of investors (of all colors). It seemed to me to be a boom time in the River North neighborhood, and things were changing rapidly.

Around June or July, my left knee started hurting. It was excruciating. I should have expected this. I was running every day, and I was working the night shift for eight hours plus the spa for at least eight hours. with very little downtime. I realized work was definitely more important, but I had paid my fee to run in the Chicago Marathon, and that was not cheap. I knew I would run; I just did not know what my strategy would be. I had never run a distance greater than a mile for military training/testing. I prayed on it. I figured God would take care of me, one way or another. He always has and always would.

It was fun listening to the *Left Behind* series that was popular at this time. I would pop in a cassette while I was driving. I was listening to WONU and other Christian stations/programming. I was no saint by any means, but listening to the programming made me feel less like a sinner.

I did additional work around the spa. I helped with the laundry, trash, small errands, etc. I felt like I was contributing to this black-owned business. Business was steadily increasing, and the word was getting out. I may have been hallucinating, but I thought I had heard Bonnie mention my name on the radio once (maybe). Anyway, I had great support from my clients.

September was here before I knew it, and stone massage was the new rage in the late 1990s. The owners offered to pay for my four-day training/certification class in Schaumburg, Illinois. I decided I would take the class but pay for it myself, just in case I had to leave this establishment, I did not want to owe anyone. When I booked the four-day class, I had no idea it started on the same Sunday as the Chicago marathon. I had not run since June or July, thinking I would save all my effort for race day. (What a stupid idea.)

I was also thinking about my exit strategy from the spa because things just weren't as close as it was in the beginning. I was wondering if the ownership had some financial issues. The vibe there was not the same, although I enjoyed the clientele.

Race day came. I was on edge. I got up and left the Y at 4:30 a.m. I could not sleep anymore. I had gotten my runner's packet the day before. I needed to get pins for my bib number (the number that runners wear). There was this convenient store downtown I went into. The morning air was chilly. The closer I got to Grant Park, the chillier it seemed to get. I saw a few other runners with their partners or crew, depending on size or sponsorship. I totally forgot about how chilly it would be before the race, so I did not have any sweats or jogging suit. I was there in my tank top, shorts, and New Balance shoes, which were recommended to me by a runner/sales associate at the Fleet Feet Store in Old Town weeks before, when I had a gait analysis. I had this tendency/habit of running on my forefoot as opposed to heel-toe. The runner/saleswoman cautioned me that could be a problem to maintain this running pattern for 26.2 miles. I guess I would find out the hard way.

Time wore on, and I was getting increasingly anxious as well as cold. It was five thirty, then five forty-five, then six o'clock. I was able to find a small open tent for the runners. I sat in one of the folding chairs and just began massaging my legs. I don't know what I intended to gain or prove by this. I knew it calmed me down and made my legs feel more relaxed, especially being exposed to the cool morning air. As other runners came in and saw what I was doing, some of them began doing the same thing. I saw people there with different flags representing their countries of origin. I would find out later the number was greater than one hundred (of the countries represented).

At about six thirty, I left the tent. There were runners everywhere and all levels of activity on Columbus drive. The elite runners were way up front and a few partitions/barriers divided the participants from the crowd. I could hear the well-wishers screaming to loved ones. There was this mass of humanity on both sides of the streets—what a crowd, a sea of humanity lifting me up. I did not let anyone know I was running this race. I just wanted to finish in under six hours and thirty minutes (so I could get a medal and get into the paper). I parked my car nearby on State Street, so I could just get in the car and go to Schaumburg after the race. The class would begin Sunday afternoon, so I had to finish in six-and-a-half hours to have enough travel time to get to Schaumburg. I figured the first day was overview/theory—no hands on. I reasoned I could be a little late.

Since I parked the car nearby, I had no alternative but to run 26.2 miles back here. I could not think of a more motivating factor at this time. Even though I had not run since June, I figured I could make it in under six-and-a-half hours. I stretched some more—the calves, the hamstrings, the quads, anything to pass the time and decrease the anxiety.

It was time to line up, get ready, set . . . ***Bang! Bang!*** the shots rang out. We were off, or so we thought. There were so many runners that in the initial moments (for us in the back), we felt more like cattle than runners. I felt locked-in for a couple of blocks, then I could feel more freedom as I ran.

I remember the station around Lincoln Park. I got some water and some Gatorade, and my legs were feeling pretty good. My focus was to finish in under six-and-a-half hours.

The marathon was a great way to showcase Chicago as a city of neighborhoods. After going through Lincoln Park, we went through Lake View then Addison Street, which would be the furthest north we would go. I knew we were close to Wrigley Field. After that, it was time to head south towards downtown again. We ran through this place nicknamed "Boystown," a popular gay neighborhood in Chicago. There were dancers, a drill team, and a very festive and flamboyant atmosphere. Each neighborhood had its own style/energy, yet they were distinctly Chicago.

We passed by Moody Bible Institute on Wells. We also went through various ethnic enclaves as we were traveling from the predominantly Northern European north side to the Italian and Greek west loop area to the African American west side by Malcolm X College. We then headed back towards the city. Running past Whitney Young, the magnet high school, I could begin to feel my legs getting heavier and heavier. I also felt like I needed to use the bathroom. We ran past UIC (University of Illinois at Chicago) and Pilsen, into Chinatown. I had gone as far north and as far west as we would go, but I had to use the bathroom now!

There were lines at the porta potties. As I waited, I could feel my legs slowly turn to lead. I rocked side to side trying to shake it off. It seemed like an eternity, but it was finally my turn. I couldn't begin to describe what I saw and smelled, so I won't. I did know I wanted to get out of that container as soon as possible without falling or touching anything. I had to keep going; my car was at the finish line.

I was over halfway done now. My trek south was the most difficult. I could not shake the heavy feeling in my legs. I could also feel a twinge in my left knee, like the volume on some audio equipment that would be slowly tweaked for the rest of this race. As I got further south and the race dragged on, the crowds got more sparse and the runners were thinning out. I am sure all the fast people were done by now, and here I was at White Sox Park (U.S. Cellular Field). The pain was quite intense in my left knee, which reduced me to a hobble/run type of gait. I had to just walk at one point, but at least now I was heading north back to Grant Park (and my car).

I was talking to a young lady from Canada whose legs were in a similar situation as mine. We walked, ran, and hobbled for a while until we got around IIT (Illinois Institute of Technology) and Michigan Avenue. I knew it was a straight shot to Grant Park—yes, it was almost twenty blocks or so away, but it was less than what I started with. I got my second wind. I was filled with renewed energy. My left knee was not convinced. The closer we got, the crowds increased, as well as my energy. The knee would only let me go for so long then I would have to walk again. It felt like a gremlin was in my knee with a jackhammer. I hoped no damage would be long-lasting—I still had a class to go to later. Remembering this caused me to push a little harder.

I was at Roosevelt Road (Twelfth Street). I hung a right, and it was an incline that took us up to Columbus Drive. I felt like I was going up a mountain. My calves ached, and my legs burned, but I was almost done. My first marathon was almost over. I finished the 26 miles—now was the 0.2 past the reviewing stands to the finish line. Painful as it was, I forced myself to run. (I could not have just walked across the finish line.) My left knee was killing me, but the claps of the crowd drowned out the pain for the moment. I had to get some of that fresh fruit past the finish line. The beer tasted like nectar/ambrosia.

I did not have time to gloat. I had to hobble my way to my car so I could drive to Schaumburg for my class. I felt the heaviness in my legs as I drove. I tried not to speed too much, but my legs felt so heavy. I was only a few minutes late. The lady was still talking about her background.

My next few days were achy, but I would get my certificate for being "Hot Stone Certified," which was another service the spa could offer. The service became quite popular in the upcoming weeks. I realized I wanted more CEUs (continuing education units) from this place, so in the upcoming weeks (on my days off), I would go a few more times. I was still working forty hours at the Home for the Developmentally Disabled on the north side.

In one of the classes, I met a young lady named Kim, who worked for a spa in the western suburbs. We talked and she mentioned that the owner was looking for a male therapist. I put this in the back of my mind since I was already working somewhere, and I still felt some loyalty to where I was presently working. The loyalty was waning. I wanted more compensation for my services.

A few weeks later, I had another class in Schaumburg. This time, the owner of the spa in Lombard (where Kim worked) came in. Her name was Angela. She was part English with an English accent. We talked for a while during the breaks of our class. I arranged a time when I could come in and give a demo of my work. I worked on her therapist. Both the therapist and the owner were impressed. I was made an offer which was a few percentage points greater than what I was getting.

I began to split my time between the two places, as well as continued my night job. I was wearing thin—I had to make a decision soon. I chose the suburbs. Although it was more of a drive, I liked the clientele and the work environment more. Although this place was not as diverse as Chicago, the patrons here had a greater disposable income– and, therefore, greater frequency in spa services, which meant an increase in income. I could save more, and I did.

The year 1999 ended; there was no apocalypse, and time moved forward. Initially, there was some hesitancy from the clientele. I think it was more because of my gender than my color (I hope). I was the only person of color working there.

Thinking back, I don't know for certain why touch had such an appeal to me. I thought about it, and a childhood memory came to mind. It was my mom reading me the Gospels (New Testament) in the form of *Good News for Modern Man*, which was a popular book when I was growing up. She would read to me at night while my dad worked the night shift at Republic Steel Mill. I remembered the story of this Jesus who could heal people just by touching them. I was so fascinated he could do this. It all came together at that moment—healing people by touch.

I felt a connection not only with my mother (now deceased) by massage, but also with the spiritual aspect of healing—the whole person, both body and spirit. Massage was more than massage to me—it was a calling, my purpose. I still felt a sense a guilt that I had not become a doctor since that is what I entered the University of Illinois to become. Maybe I would become a doctor later. Right now, I was satisfied with people leaving feeling better than before.

I was so fortunate to have attended Seattle Massage School (later Ashmead College). The emphasis was on the therapist, which meant a focus on proper posture, body mechanics, and technique and wellness. How could a therapist give a great massage (continually) if they were out of balance physically, mentally, emotionally or spiritually? One of my earliest teachers of Swedish massage was Norwegian. I believe she was from a neighborhood called Ballard in Seattle (which was once heavily Scandinavian). Annie (my teacher) was a practitioner of a movement therapy called Feldenkrais. She walked us through a number of sequences. I learned such great posture here. I felt as if I could massage all day without tiring.

In 2000, I wanted to increase my tech knowledge and possibly get a new career. I took an A+ certification/training class at Malcolm X College on the west side (in addition to my two jobs). I passed the certification class, and I passed the test to be A+ certified. I reduced my hours at the spa. I interviewed with IBM and got the job.

Although I decreased my hours at the spa, I did not quit. Angela was not happy, but she seemed understanding. All along I was searching for something, yet not quite finding it, but now I would be working in IT—how ironic.

I worked a few small jobs in Downtown and in the Chicago land area. The big break came. It was to install computers in a nuclear power plant southwest of Chicago. I took a nuclear power tech training course at the Braidwood Plant in Braidwood, Illinois. I passed. I felt I was on track. I felt I was moving in the right direction. It was early 2000. I was entering a tech field working for IBM. Everything was moving upward. What could happen?

A friend of my brother Ted left a note at the spa in Chicago for me to call her, in reference to my brother. I hope he had not died or relapsed. I called the friend, and she wanted me to call my brother, but she could not be specific as to why. From the tone of her voice, I knew something had to be wrong. I decided to forget about the past and give him a call. My brother sounded calm, but I could tell he was upset. His fiancé and child had moved out. He was in an abusive marriage that he was getting himself out of via divorce. He asked me to come back. I thought about it for a moment. I thought about what I would be giving up financially and career-wise, and I thought about the trips to the doctors and helping with therapy. I paused. I then said yes. I guess sometimes blood is thicker than water.

In this instant, my life again reversed itself. Although I enjoyed learning the technical information, I could not do that and help my brother at the same time. I made up an excuse to be polite to IBM—I told them that I was hired by a competitor. (I did not think they or anyone else would understand me leaving to help care for a relative.)

My old routine was reinstated. I would work nights at the Home for the Developmentally Disabled and the days at the spa. I explained to the owner of the spa my brother's condition, and that I might need flexibility in scheduling. She agreed. It was a juggling act. My brother had good days and bad. There would be new medications and therapies he would try with varying results.

The year 2001 came and so did September 11. I remember exactly what I was doing. I was driving south on Lake Shore Drive after my night shift. I heard the announcement right around Navy Pier. The broadcast on the radio was so surreal. It reminded me of Orson Welles's *The War of the Worlds*, but this was for real.

Could I believe this was happening now, planes crashing into buildings? I was examining Chicago's skyline, wondering if we were next. It was real in real-time. President Bush was in his first term. This was his first test. His popularity before this point was not so good. It's very interesting what a national tragedy can do in terms of presidential support.

We were in the process of moving to a larger spa near Yorktown Center Mall in Lombard, Illinois. The owner was concerned, as other businesses were, about how this would affect business and about the big picture—how this would affect the economy and our country.

We moved into the new spa called Simply Beautiful in November. Angela was concerned, but we did well. I am sure Angela was thinking, "What have I done?" She was always careful about business decisions, but no one could have predicted this. Who was this Osama Bin Laden, and what would be our response as a nation? I had Muslim friends, and some of my clients were Muslim. The western suburbs have a great number of Muslims. I guess the only thing to do now was wait.

The grand opening of the new spa came. It was a roaring success. I was concerned as well, being the only African American and male that worked at the spa. Would my career/business suffer due to other people's intolerance? I must say "not so", for I had a number of people come to me. I would guess greater than 90 percent of my clientele were white women in their thirties or above. Business was getting better, and I had my regulars that came over from the old spa, which was now closed. Life moved on. Fall moved in.

It was a particularly cold and frosty night. I was on my way to my night job. I had the right of way, but the other car did not stop, and I was hit on my front end. Ironically, my older vehicle with heavy mileage was operable; theirs was not and had to be towed from the scene. The young ladies had to be taken home by the police. I had close to three hundred thousand miles on the vehicle.

I was able to make it to work and made it through the shift. The insurance company totaled out my Sentra, and I received a nice check to purchase a 2001 Jeep Cherokee. It had a little over twenty thousand miles on the vehicle. The jeep was perfect for my needs. It was ideal for transporting my brother and the wheelchair. I definitely needed it for the upcoming winter.

I visited my children around Christmas. It was even more fun than the first time. They were well and getting bigger. My daughter was playing the French horn. She played me a few selections she had been practicing. Time just seemed to fly, and it was time to return and prepare for 2002. What a year it turned out to be.

Little Teddy's mom started allowing little Ted to come visit, and we had a great time. He was very energetic, like his dad was when he was his age. He was four now, and a joy to have around. We would go out to breakfast on Sundays at a local Denny's. It was fun and interesting to see the similarities in behavior between father and son.

I was lucky that summer because my children were in a nearby suburb visiting their aunt. I figured my children could meet their cousin little Ted and see their uncle Ted. There were numerous visits. I did not want the summer to end. To see our children together was great.

Before my children visited, we had a visit from my sister Dee, who lived in Denver. She came around Memorial Day and stayed a few days.

We went to Chicago to see the sites, visit Dad's grave, and just hang out. This was turning out to be a great year with all these unexpected visits. It seemed too good to be true. It was.

My brother died suddenly at home, the home that we with our parents built on land that was purchased by my grandfather, Samuel Farnsworth Bethel. My little brother was dead at thirty. I had just turned forty. The cause was related to his multiple sclerosis, which had become more aggressive. In fact, while my kids were there, a few weeks before, they visited their Uncle Ted at Rush Hospital.

I thought things were getting better, and now he was gone. It was the end of the family I grew up closest with. My father, my mother, and now my little brother was gone; I was the only one left. At least I had my other siblings: Dana, Sam and Dee. I also had my children: Brianna, Brian, and Brandon. I also had my nephews: little Ted, Tony, and Donny, and my only niece, Alisha.

My sisters were a big help in planning the funeral and helping me and little Ted through the initial grieving process. After the funeral, I had to find something to focus on besides work, now that my brother was gone. I continued to see Teddy on Sundays for breakfast at Denny's. It was not the same, but we enjoyed each other's company. I still worked two jobs to stay busy. I even took a third job as a physical therapist assistant to take my mind off my brother, but it wasn't enough. I had to find something else to focus on.

I decided I would run another marathon. I ran in the house on a wooden floor. I had a better routine this time and more space to run. The marathon would be for my brother Ted. I worked my two jobs and saw Teddy when I could. He was going to be in kindergarten in the fall—I could not wait. I had also met someone from work, and we were spending a great amount of time with one another.

Race day came. I wore sweats this time so I could remove them when I got too warm. I still had shorts on underneath. I planned the race better. I had a better diet. I used supplements now. I had used them on and off since the military. I found them to be quite useful in a number of situations. When I was in high school, college, and the military, I read books by Dr. Earl Mindell, who was a registered pharmacist and expert on nutrition and supplements. One supplement that was particularly popular at this time was Glucosamine with Chondroitin for the joints. I began taking it after my first marathon in 1999. I thought I would not run distance races ever again. I felt Glucosamine worked for me. I would not have used it if I had a seafood allergy.

Although I was not a doctor at this time, I had clients as a massage therapist who had issues with their joints due to wear and tear over the years, arthritis, and other conditions. My clients knew I had run a marathon before and that I was going to run again in the fall. Since I was so adamant about not running again after the 1999 race, my clients wanted to know what changed my mind. I told them Glucosamine with Chondroitin and MSM. I told them it might be a placebo effect at work, and I warned them not to take it if they have a seafood allergy. They should also check with their doctor/health care provider first. I told them I used the more expensive brand and that they should not do this cheaply.

I was surprised at how many people took the supplement. I was even more surprised at my elderly/senior clients and the athletes I worked on. I had one triathlete who told me she noticed the difference within a couple of weeks (I even doubted this). I told them they had to be compliant with the instructions on the bottle (most often ninety days of consistent usage initially). I remember noticing my results around two-and-a-half to three months after, which was close to the recommended time. The older clients had the patience to go the distance. The athletes had the discipline to complete the three-month trial period. I made sure I was not promising, promoting, or proselytizing anything—I just wanted my clients to get better. I was also adamant about them checking with their doctor since I was not one (at this time). I had a few people who had no results. I had only one negative result, and that was because the person was not listening when I told her not to use the product if she had a shellfish allergy. Even then, it was more discomfort than sickness.

My runs got better and better. I also became more interested in health, wellness, and nutrition to complement massage therapy. I definitely saw a difference in my clientele that believed in a holistic mind-body approach as opposed to those clients that were more rigid and dogmatic. A number of my clients had followed the work of Andrew Weil and/or Deepak Chopra. I also noticed my clients that had some type of spiritual belief; whether it was Christianity, Islam, Buddhist, Hindu, Judaism, or any other belief were more resilient and open to try new techniques/suggestions. From my family history, I remember my great-great-grandmother Caroline being a healer and how she was asked to go to a nearby plantation to help with a small pox outbreak. She utilized the knowledge of herbs, teas, and the like that her Mother Nidra from Africa taught her.

I became more interested in the alternative medicine field. I had worked with three chiropractors up to this point. I saw firsthand the work that we did worked on the patients. I saw our successes; it was more than our failures. One of the chiropractors I worked with wanted me to become one. The type of adjustment did not suit me. I believed if I could decrease the tension in the muscle through massage, stretching, and nutrition, I could decrease the forces applied to the skeletal system. Over time, the person self-adjusted. If they added certain modalities, postural exercises, and strengthened the weaker/imbalanced muscles, they could maintain their "adjustment" for even a greater period of time. I had dreams about this, but I had no knowledge of what naprapathy was or what a naprapath did (at this time).

Race day came. The 2003 Chicago Marathon was a go. I was ready this time. I finished the race a few minutes faster than 1999—not bad, considering I had not trained at all until October of 2002. I felt my brother Ted was watching and was with me all the way. That marathon was for him. I had no pain in the knees. I walked with a normal gait (step)—no limping. If the Glucosamine Chondroitin and MSM was a placebo, this was the best placebo my clients and I had.

Not too long after the race, I received a flyer about something called naprapathy, which I had never heard of before. It sounded interesting. I wondered maybe this was what my dreams were about. I put it off and ignored it because I did not have the money. I threw the flyer away.

I continued to work two jobs, run, see my girlfriend, and see my nephew when I could. He was growing so fast, and his personality was rambunctious, like his dad was at that age. Ted's mom got him into football to give him focus and discipline like my parents had for my brother. From the very beginning, my brother was the fastest on the team. There were only three or four African American kids on the team. The coaches were fair and played people according to their talent as well as rotating people to see their strengths and weaknesses.

My brother Ted was an excellent running back and led the Momence team to a few local championships. I was very happy that little Ted would also be playing football. When my brother was playing football, at the practice sessions the other kids on the team would try to get a sip out of my brother's water jug because they believed his water was special. They believed since we lived in the rural/farm area, somehow the water was better. My father was actually involved with the football team as a volunteer (as he had been when I was in elementary school). My brother's talent on the football field was much greater than mine. My father (posthumously) received a plaque for his service to the football team. I even assistant coached the B team before I left to enter the navy.

These memories of the past kept me going as I was running around the house. I felt no pain in my knees. I was wondering if the Glucosamine worked for me what other supplements I could try to improve my performance. I just kept this in my mind for now because I did not have a specific problem to work on, and I did not want it to seem like a placebo. I wanted to take a specific supplement to receive a specific result (i.e., the Glucosamine Chondroitin with MSM for my joint pain).

Chapter Nine

The year 2004 was here. Time sure does fly. It had been twenty years since I met my children's mother. My kids were no longer kids. They would be seventeen, sixteen, and fourteen this year. Their mom had long since moved back to Washington State and was living a brand new life with great friends and a wonderful support system. My children were in the church. They were learning Christian values and I was so happy for them. Our distance did not change my love for them. They inspired me.

I received another one of those postcards about naprapathy in the mail. I held on to this one and went to a demonstration at a school in Chicago on the northwest side. This area was predominantly Eastern European (Polish mostly), Latino (mostly Mexican), with some African Americans and Asians. I never realized that the originator of this field of medicine had at one point been one of the first students of chiropractic medicine. Oakley Smith was a chiropractor before he founded naprapathy. With Smith's focus on connective tissue instead of skeletal structure, my old dreams came to mind. This is what I was dreaming about all those years ago in Seattle, when I worked with Dr. Clark—I just did not know about it. I enjoyed the demo given by Dr. Lavonne Hill. The history and application of naprathy for connective disorders fascinated me. I like the concise definition of Dorland's Illustrated Medical Dictionary, Thirty-first Edition: "naprapathy: a system of therapy employing manipulation of connective tissue (ligaments, muscles, and joints) and dietary measures; said to facilitate the recuperative and regenerative processes of the body."

There was still this issue of lacking money. I had a friend from my night job who was very supportive of my ideas and enjoyed reading my poetry that I had now published and had books available. I told her my situation. She gave me the money to begin. Ironically, she and my brother were both born on March 5. This was too weird because my brother Ted enjoyed my poetry as well. I guess I had no more excuses.

Classes started in the fall of 2004. The marathon would also be that fall in October. I was so psyched up I could not contain myself. I felt like this was a mandate from the Creator, giving me this opportunity. I would now at least have an opportunity to become a doctor (at last). The title would be doctor of naprapathic medicine, naprapath, or DN. I now had another goal and another reason to praise God—although I praised him all along.

I started one of my favorite classes in September—anatomy. The joy of this class was that it would be working with cadavers at Rush Hospital near Downtown Chicago. Our instructor was Dr. Beck, DN. Although demanding, he was very knowledgeable, and I understood his reasoning. We were taught about the functions and systems of the human body, the locations of the parts, and how it operates as a whole. We would endure three semesters of Dr. Beck—I could not have been happier.

When I ran the marathon in 2004, I shaved a few more minutes off my time, and I could not wait for the next marathon in 2005, which would be my fourth. Life was full of study and work, and I did not mind one bit. My daughter would turn eighteen this year, and the same friend that helped me with my first payment had connections in the fashion industry. My friend had a beautiful gown made for my daughter's prom. There was no way I could pay this friend back. I just thought it was so weird the time she came into my life and the fact that my brother Ted and her were born on the same day.

My older sister Dana had been distance running in the Denver area and wanted to know if we could run the next Chicago Marathon together. I happily agreed and purchased our spots for the race. I trained even harder now, not to beat my sister but to keep pace with her. Since she and my other siblings lived around the Denver area, I figured she would have a slight advantage over me due to the increase in altitude. My older sister had not run a marathon before, but she was very studious about preparation and her nutrition.

I was still working on my core curriculum as a naprapath before the classes which would focus on the charting and the naprapathic adjustment. These classes would come much later. I did well in organic chemistry, biochemistry, and rehab principles, a number of techniques I was familiar with when I was working in the physical therapy field.

Training for the marathon was fun. I was looking forward to seeing my sister again. I remember my sister arriving with her boyfriend Greg. The first thing we did was to see little Ted. She loved seeing her nephew, and the feeling was mutual. We arrived at the hotel later that Friday night. Saturday morning we received our running packets from McCormick Place, and stayed with some of my sister's cousins for a while.

Then it was downtown to the runner's dinner at the Palmer House. Over 120 countries where represented. We saw people there from all over. The ballroom was magnificent. The speakers were electrifying and inspirational. My sister was briefly interviewed by one of the crew from one of the local news stations. (She is very photogenic and positive.) The meal had a lot of carbs (think spaghetti and garlic bread). A beer was offered—I definitely accepted. We slept well that night, anticipating the race in the morning.

The day started extra early for us since our hotel was on the south side near Midway Airport. We got into the downtown area while it was still dark—I believe at around five or five thirty in the morning. We parked in a very convenient place so we could pull out immediately after the race and get to State Street, which is so ironic because I parked near this spot for my very first marathon.

We followed a crowd of runners to Grant Park. We admired the back of a young girl's T-shirt which read "our sport is your sport's punishment." I thought that was very clever, considering all the laps I ran when I wrestled in high school. It did not help that our wrestling coach was also the coach for cross-country and endurance was favored over strength. We ran after practice, so it did feel like a punishment. Come to think of it, we ran laps for tennis and football, too. I guess the little girl's T-shirt was right.

My sister's boyfriend Greg was definitely supportive of her. He took pictures, held her stuff, and gave her words of encouragement/advice. The time came for us to enter the corral—that is what I called the fenced in area for the runners. My sister seemed nervous and giddy at the same time. Her enthusiasm has always been infectious.

The gun went off—the race was on. We kept pace with each other and were enjoying each other's company for the first half of the race.

After the halfway point, I could feel her pulling away—slowly at first, then it was very visible, then to the point where I could no longer see her. At that point, I knew she was ahead so I did not have to be concerned that she would not complete the race. We were running two separate races now. I was just focused on finishing, knowing my sister would finish (since she was ahead). I was wondering how many minutes she would beat me by. I wasn't hurting or achy at all. I felt in good condition. It was a routine marathon for me.

I finished a few minutes faster, but I did not break the six-hour mark—somewhere after 6:10 and before 6:15. To my amazement, my sister had only beaten me by a few minutes—I believe her time was around 6:08. I thought that wasn't too bad, since she had trained at a higher altitude. She invited me to run in Denver. I did not think it wise due to the altitude difference, especially since I would be training in flat Chicago and running a marathon in the "Mile High City."

After the race, we all had a great meal at TGI Friday's, and the next day we did a little sightseeing, which included Millennium Park. It seemed so new, a novelty worth seeing. Dana and Greg enjoyed it. When I see my sister and her boyfriend, I see a beautiful couple that loves each other. I don't see black and white, and no one else noticed either. Maybe the world is changing. I hated to see them go.

I had my fourth marathon under my belt. Classes were going well and so was work. While my sister was here, I asked her certain questions about family since she was the oldest. She answered them the best she could. Since we had different mothers, we had different experiences, but we both loved our father and our family.

I received an article of mail at this time about studying tuina (Chinese massage) in Beijing, China. The stationary looked official. I knew a colleague that had gone years before, and they had a great learning experience. I received a letter before, but I had tossed it out. I don't know why this time the same exact letter intrigued me, but it did. I thought this would be a chance to further my education in Traditional Chinese Medicine (TCM). I would be exposed to something new. Maybe this instruction would enhance my own training. I would also get a chance to visit Far East Asia since I already visited Asia Minor and the Middle East.

I decided to go for it. I talked with some colleagues, some seemed interested as well. I worked extra hard to save up money for this trip.

One of my older colleagues at the college who was also named Tony said it would be great. He was already an acupuncturist and a teacher at one of the local schools of Oriental medicine.

The fact that I had not finished the marathon in under six hours kept eating at me. I had to give it one last try. I knew I would be out of the country a month before the race. I reasoned if I trained hard to the end of August, the two weeks in China in early September would not affect me running a marathon in October. We'll see. I was really determined this time, especially after running with my sister.

It was now 2006. My children would be nineteen, eighteen, and sixteen this year. Brianna would graduate high school and go to college. I could not wait for her graduation. My work, school, and personal life were all in balance. Teddy was doing well in football. I was taking him to Sylvan to help improve his classroom skills. He was becoming more well-rounded. I bought him a guitar he wanted, and he practiced. He was also in the school band and played the trumpet. He was developing quite nicely.

My trip to China was getting closer, I had never had a passport before; it was an adventure just to get one of those things. I was so excited I did not mind the paperwork. I guess being after 9/11 the process was probably more detailed.

I was concerned about going away to China for two weeks and not training. The months seemed to slip away. There was still a lot of theory in class. No adjustments yet. I was focused on work and getting to China. All thirty of us received instructional packets that covered what we would be doing in China: some Chinese words, etiquette, protocol, and past experiences of some of the participants. I was getting into the adventure. Thinking about what it would be like at the Great Wall, the Forbidden City, and Tiananmen Square.

The week finally came. I had made all my arrangements for work to be in China. There was a flight from Chicago to LA and from LA to Korea for refueling, then on to Beijing. I believe the trip altogether from Chicago to Beijing took seventeen hours. The flight carrier was Asiana. It was top-notch for customer service and comfort. I had not enjoyed flying like this since the 1970s. The women were in uniforms. Everyone was kind and courteous. I did not want to leave.

We arrived in South Korea for refueling. There was time to look around the airport. We decided to try some traditional Korean food at a nice sit-down place in the airport. The food was spicy but good. It felt good to walk around and stretch the legs. The airport was so clean. Not so much as a scrap of paper was on the floor.

We were back on the plane in a short while. The seats were as comfortable as they were before. We got into China in the early afternoon. We got our things settled at our respective hotels. There was time for shopping at a bustling Beijing Market. We also had our first meal in China at a great noodle place—I really enjoyed it. One thing about this meal (and others I would have later) was that there was not a lot of meat—it was used mostly as a side rather than a main course. The emphasis was more on the rice and vegetables than the meat.

The next day, we would begin our classes at the Dang Zhuan Hospital in Beijing. We would learn the basics of TCM as well as the medical applications of tuina. Tuina is used with the energy channels of the body and the five element theory (which I won't get into here). In the morning, we would visit the hospital and observe the treatments given by the doctors. In the afternoon, we would have class on medical tuina techniques and their application and theory.

After our session on Friday, we began our first weekend in Beijing. We had an epic banquet with the Chinese instructors and interpreters. The people were very hospitable and polite. We had a birthday celebration as well for all those born in September (which I happened to be a part of—I was born on September 4). It was such a bustling time in China as they were preparing for something called the Moon Festival, which was a seasonal holiday. Certain baked goods were being made for purchase at the local bakeries.

During the weekend, we first visited the Forbidden City, which had several hundred years of history. We also visited the Temple of Heaven and Tiananmen Square, the largest city square in the world. The next day, we went to the Great Wall. What an experience. How majestic. How powerful. The wall went on for miles, but we only had a small access to it (a couple of miles). You could walk up the winding stairs or take a cable car up or down. Another option (for going down) was a winding toboggan chute—a plastic toboggan on a metal chute. I took the chute down; it was fast and fun.

It was a marvel to walk along the top of the wall. The width was about the size of four horsemen riding across/abreast. I believe that was intentional in case of warding off intruders, which was why the wall was built in the first place. I believe it is also the only manmade structure (that I know of) that is visible from the moon. Some people also believe that it is the longest graveyard, since when the workers died, they made no graves for them. They were just dumped along the wall (so we were told).

There were vendors going both up and down the hill by the Great Wall, which we had to walk up and down to get to the wall. They could be very convincing, although the markup could be quite significant.

We had brought sack lunches and ate them on top of the wall. The air was warm and calm. The view was fantastic. The clouds looked like funny-shaped silkworms, with the royal blue sky as background.

The time came to leave, and my legs were a little tight from all the walking. I felt like running, but I knew the marathon would come around soon enough. We had been so busy in the classroom learning the previous week—this was the first time I had even thought of running while in China.

We got back on our buses. We also visited the third largest jade distributor in Asia (which is what we were told). I did not have any idea of all the different types of or qualities of, or colors of, or properties of jade. It was overwhelming and fascinating. I wanted to buy so much (which was what they wanted), but I had so little—I was happy about that. I purchased a few items for my children. I was very glad when we left that place (I had to use such self-control).

The next day was Monday, and we had one last week of learning. I was already figuring out ways I could incorporate the techniques I was learning to fit into treatment sessions. I was enjoying the theory as well as the application. Time passed so quickly.

There was so much construction going on. The city was preparing for the 2008 Olympics. Since I knew the director of this tuina program and he was well connected with the Chinese, my hope was to possibly be a therapist for the Beijing Olympics in 2008. We seemed to have a good rapport with one another. We were both born in the Year of the Tiger, although he was twelve years older and lived in a suburb neighboring my old town of Evanston, Illinois.

The week came to an end much too fast, and there was a final banquet and farewells to our instructors and interpreters. There was an exchanging of gifts and cultures. The world felt smaller while I was there. These people would definitely be people I would want to be friends with. It made me wonder about the world situation. Why can't we just all get along?

The morning came soon enough. Bags were packed, and hugs were exchanged. It was off to the airport for our seventeen-hour flight back to Chicago. I slept a great deal on the way back. The programming and the films were not quite as interesting as going over. Maybe I was a little tired from the past two exciting weeks.

I got back home wanting to try these new techniques the Chinese have been using for over one thousand years. I infused it into my work as everything else and applied it therapeutically, depending on the client's condition. I always did an intake first, so all my treatments were based on the individual's present condition. My clients seemed to enjoy the additions to the regular treatments. The influx of business kept me busy, and I was able to get back into running the few weeks left before the marathon. I was not as rusty as I thought. The race day came. I had been using my Glucosamine and Chondroitin with MSM religiously since after my marathon in 1999. I believe by now it had developed into something more than a placebo, and so did my clients.

Race day for the 2006 Chicago Marathon was quite a sight. It was also chilly, the coldest start in its twenty-nine-year history. (Ironically, the next year would be the hottest.) The events did make me think about the possibility/reality of climate change. My body seemed to be acclimating well to the weather.

I was running with a timed group. Our goal was five hours and forty-five minutes. If I made it, it would be my first marathon in under six hours. I was so psyched up. I was hoping I could keep up. This was my first time running with a group. There is strength in unity. I did everything my group did when they did it. When they slowed, I slowed. When they fast walked, I fast walked. When they ran, I ran. For me, the toughest part was the walking. I would fall almost to the end of the group during the walking phase. When the running phase came, I went to the head of the pack. It was this yo-yo effect, yet there was a consistency to it, and we were on schedule almost the whole race. I don't know if it was being a part of a group or the adrenaline or both, but I was not as tired as I was in past marathons. We were doing well. I even sped ahead of the leader at the finish line for a 5:44 finish. I did it! Finally. The apples and the beer at the finish area were so refreshing.

Not too long after the race, I received a letter for a 2007 trip to Beijing. I would have an opportunity to be assigned to the National Olympic Training Center. I was excited. Could this be the opportunity I had been waiting for to make it to the 2008 Olympics? I guess I would have to go to find out.

The beginning of 2007 came. All was progressing nicely at work. Money was being saved. I was getting all my paperwork together for the trip, but I had some unexpected bills for my car and other expenses. Suddenly, I did not have enough money to go to Beijing, and I had been saving rather well. Time was just ticking away, and I wondered if I was going to miss my opportunity. My funds were getting lower and lower. I thought I might miss the deadline. I had saved a certain amount in reserve to go to my son Brian's high school graduation in Washington State. I could not touch that money. My credit was bad. I always had great friends and paid them back, but this was a fairly large sum of money. I had to do this. I had no choice; I was too close to my goal. I had to ask my friend.

She was a friend and colleague I had traveled with to China last year. She would not be able to go, but she loaned me the money. I was going to go. I still had a chance (maybe) to be a therapist for Beijing. I submitted my application under the deadline. My spot for the 2007 trip to Beijing was secure. All was right in the world—or so I thought.

The time was around March and I was getting happy about another one of my children graduating from high school, Brian. I was thinking about all the fun we would have and the fact I had not seen my children in a while. I received a phone call from the director of the program for the trip to Beijing. I was wondering, "What could it be now?" The director of the program had a secure spot for the 2008 Beijing Olympics—I was so happy for him. He was giving me an opportunity. He said if I would go on the trip in June instead of the September trip, I would have a greater chance of making the 2008 Olympics. I understood his hint, but I thought about how the time frame was the same as my son's graduation. We had always stressed education is freedom. My family had always stressed education even in slavery. Although I wanted to go so bad, I could not let my son down. I could not miss my son's high school graduation. The director understood. He had three high-achieving sons himself. I would still go to China in 2007; maybe I would get lucky anyway. I belonged to a group called the sixth ring, which is a group of people who fund the American Olympic athletes. I thought it would be quite the story to make it to an Olympics myself.

The remaining months to China passed so quickly. The flight was as comfortable as before. I felt so focused this time. The trip was a professional one for me now. I wanted to be known for my skills. I saw the sites last time. I was thinking maybe I still had a chance. I got a chance to work more intensely with the instructors. I had a chance to use my limited Mandarin (only a few words). I made a few friends. I had my own patient load for tuina treatments of Chinese nationals. I did not get a chance to work on any Olympians, but I did work at the National Olympic Training Center, and I had time to interact with the doctors that worked with the athletes. I was fortunate to see some of the athletes (from a distance—security was tight).

The second trip to the Great Wall seemed routine, but the view was just as magnificent and the sky just as brilliant as the first time. Olympics or not, it was worth the trip. I definitely showed more restraint at the Jade Palace. I also had a chance to celebrate my birthday at a popular night club; I believe it was called A Fun Ti. It was great being onstage and interacting with the MC and other guests. We played an assortment of games and witnessed great acrobatic and dance performances.

My birthday and my trip were fantastic. Although I did not get a chance to go to the 2008 Olympics, I knew I made the right decision to see my son walk across the stage and get his diploma—what a sight. It filled my heart with such joy, another Black man with a diploma in hand. He had received a scholarship from a prestigious school of design in Southern California. I believe the initials were FIDM.

Traveling to China and learning tuina in a medical and sports environment gave me more confidence in my own skills, especially after working on Chinese Nationals that told me *hĕn hăo* or "very good" in Mandarin. I figured I could possibly incorporate what I learned in China with what I would learn in the upcoming hands-on portion of naprapathic training.

In 2009, my son Brandon graduated from high school with honors. I was so pleased. My credit was not good enough to send him to his preferred school (Howard University). My son did not let that deter him. He worked over the summer and early fall and started at Western Washington University at Bellingham, Washington. The area of business is what interested Brandon. That discipline (business) would be his focus. Brandon would be my inspiration as I entered my final stage of naprapathic study—the clinic.

Chapter Ten

In 2010, I entered the naprapathic clinic (finally). Through various twists and turns, both academically and financially, I have made it. I had my own treatment room with my own name plate:

Tony Bethel
Naprapathic Intern

We treated people from all walks of life, from the homeless to a trader at CBOT (Chicago Board of Trade) to an opera singer at the Lyric Opera House and other people in between. Their confidence in me and naprapathic medicine increased my skill level and confidence. Although I was an intern, people were calling me Doctor, as if I had been doing this for years. I took their trust very seriously. I had gotten through my academic and practical studies with almost a straight A average. (I did get a B in histology). What I got in a class did not matter now. What mattered was if I could assess the situation, take care of the problem, and involve the patient in their own health care process.

I wanted the patients to be proactive in their treatment because to me, that would give a greater probability of compliance with the treatment. I had completed three semesters of nutrition in the program, but it was so frustrating to hear from certain individuals that they didn't have the money to buy the supplements I was recommending. I always tried to be positive and creative, giving them ideas about different foods or herbs/spices they could try. I also cautioned them they would have to be more patient since the meals would not be as concentrated as a supplement. Some people were compliant, others were not.

For the year, I had more than four hundred patients. A number of these people returned at various times: weekly, bi-weekly, monthly, quarterly, etc. They came in based on their treatment schedule and/or medical insurance, benefits, or other forms of reimbursement. It was a good feeling to see people leave in a better state of mind and a better frame of body. The "mind-body" connection could not be overlooked. A number of people were dealing with pressure from the fallout of the financial crisis (i.e., layoffs, firings, mortgages, car payments, as well as physical injuries).

We were dealing with the physical, intellectual, emotional, spiritual, and financial stressors of the individual—in one word, life. A great number of our patients were very spiritual. I noticed a large number of Catholics. I remember the words of Fr. Kicanas—then Rector Kicanas, now Bishop Kicanas—"We must develop the physical, intellectual, emotional and spiritual to be well-rounded." I would like to add financial, but back in high school when you were living with your parents and going to a Catholic school, financial wasn't too hard for most families. We were working class but made do with what we had.

I may not have become a priest, but this was my congregation. I really enjoyed when a person came in and said they got a benefit from a particular exercise, or nutritional recommendation, or positive results from a modality like E-Stim or ultrasound, laser, or a particularly successful adjustment/release. I would like to share one letter of a patient sent to the clinic—to the director of the clinic. (I will only use the last initial for confidentiality.) This person came in on a regular basis throughout my tenure as an intern and when I became a licensed doctor of naprapathic medicine.

March 13, 2012

To Whom It May Concern:

This is a reference letter for Dr. Anthony Bethel. My name is Mrs. Judith H., Senior Citizen. Dr. Bethel has been my Therapist at the Naprapath Institution and School of Chicago, IL for the past one and a half years. I highly recommend Dr. Bethel since due to his care and patience I am able to lead a very normal life.

I have been afflicted with Rheumatoid Arthritis and Fibromyalgia for many years, yet since, Dr. Bethel has been giving me therapy, I have been feeling very good with little discomfort. Dr. Bethel's treatment does not stop at the office; he is always recommending exercises, healthy eating and an overall healthy life. As a matter of fact, under his guidance I have joined a health club and I feel just great.

There have been times when I've arrived for treatment not feeling my very best due to pain and fatigue; however, by the time I leave the office, I feel very good and energized. Dr Bethel will be an asset to any employer in the medical field.

Sincerely yours,
Mrs. Judith H.

Cc: Dr Taylor, Chairman and Directors of the Naprapath Institute

I was humbled by this letter and other compliments by other patients. I enjoyed being a naprapath, but I missed massage therapy.

For our naprapathic training, we had regular lectures on different developments in the field (presently) as well as in the fields of rehabilitation and western medicine. We also had a few lectures and demonstrations of acupressure and other Eastern techniques. I felt I was getting a well-rounded exposure to medicine period—not Eastern or Western, just objective, scientific, common sense healing.

In February 2011, I visited Western Washington University (WWU) to see my son Brandon get accepted into a prestigious fraternity in business based on academic and personal accomplishment (Sigma Iota Epsilon). Brandon was the only African American inductee. I was so pumped up.

The night before the induction, there was a major snowstorm in the Western Washington/Seattle area, and a number of the roads were impassable or excessively icy. No one told me (or God). I purchased a rental car to take me from the Seattle-Tacoma area to Bellingham,

Washington (about fifty miles south of the Canadian border). A number of times, I was the only vehicle on the road. I was traveling on I-5 at about thirty to thirty-five miles per hour on a major highway which was covered with packed ice/snow. (I am so glad I grew up driving in the Midwest.) There were a few slick spots, but I never spun out or lost control of the vehicle.

I made it to Bellingham in the wee hours of the morning (more like 4:00–5:00 a.m.). I had time for a few hours of sleep at the motel that I reserved a room at. I was able to take Brandon out to breakfast before his midmorning class. We talked about his future plans. He applied for an internship with a major Northwest retail chain, which he would later be selected to work at post-graduation. This smiling young man sitting in front of me had so much promise, and I was remembering when he used to sit on the pot watching *The Price is Right*, screaming out numbers with glee (like the rest of the participants).

My son Brian was working his way up the ladder at Forever 21, later to go to White House Black Market. My daughter Brianna, who had gone to Earlham in Richmond, Indiana, was to take another route and serve her country in the military.

After having a grand induction ceremony, we had hors d'oeuvres and drinks with the other inductees as well as staff and faculty. They were not only impressed that I came in from Chicago (the most distant of the guests), but how I also braved the snowstorm the previous night to be there. I did not have time to gloat. I had to leave so I could take another flight out back to Chicago. Brandon and I said our goodbyes. I was hoping the roads would be better going back to Seattle; luckily, they were. I had time to arrange a late dinner with my other son, Brian, at the pier in downtown Seattle before I would go on to the airport and have a less hectic flight home.

I don't think I was a particularly good father. I do believe that God, with the help of my children's mom, as well as family and friends, helped guide my children's path. The boys (now men) and my daughter (now a woman) did attend church in Washington when their mom moved from Southern California years ago. I believe the church helped with the formation of their values and actions. I believe now that their values and actions were forged through their faith, my faith, and their mom's faith. I believe we were all being richly rewarded/blessed.

When I got back to Chicago, I was reenergized to complete the program. Over the course of a year in the clinic, I treated people from five different continents—of all races, religions, genders, and orientations. I got the true meaning of humanity and purpose. I also received a major hand injury in September that I did not tell my instructors nor my colleagues. I was overworked. Between my three jobs that I worked outside of the clinic to put myself through, I was getting limited and irregular sleep. I was falling asleep at the wheel, and I wasn't even texting.

At the Institution for the Developmentally Disabled, I worked a forty-hour night shift per week. I worked at least twenty hours at the spa, the chiropractor on Mondays, and the remainder of the time at the naprapathic clinic. I barely had time to eat, sleep, and bathe. The overuse of my hands was killing me. I got into so many near accidents when I was driving. Between the manual adjustments and massage therapy, I was feeling an increase in pain.

I tried certain Thai techniques to help stretch people out and prepare them for the adjustment. I was still in pain/in denial. For the first time in my forty-nine years, I was having blood pressure issues (i.e., 140+/90+). This was September—would I ever make it to November to complete the program? Only a couple of my colleagues knew about my increase in blood pressure, but no one knew about the trouble in my hands.

I turned forty-nine on September 4. I had planned a surprise birthday party for one of my relatives (uncle by marriage), who was the last elder living in Covington, Tennessee. His name was Lonnie Craig, and he would be turning ninety-four on our birthday, September 4. He and my aunt Katie (his wife) had always been a great inspiration. He and his brother Giles Craig started Craig's Barbecue in Covington, Tennessee. This business had begun when there was still widespread segregation in the South. The business would last for forty years. My uncle was also a farmer and had a store by his house he and Aunt Katie operated. The Barbecue Pit was one of the first black-owned businesses in Covington and had white and black patrons.

My uncle Lonnie still drove at ninety-four and lived by himself since Aunt Katie had been gone since the mid-1980s. We both enjoyed the party and people telling their fond memories of my uncle Lonnie. Some did mention about their hospitality and being able to find refuge in a sea of segregation. I figured if my uncle could deal with the segregation of the nineteen forties and fifties, the pain I was going through was nothing.

I returned from my Labor Day holiday with more resolve to finish the program in November. I remembered two colleagues at this time— one black, one white—both naprapaths who had died roughly one year apart. Both men had died within the last year or two, and were both in their midfifties. They both had heart and/or cardiovascular issues. I was only forty-nine, but my father died at forty-seven, and my mother had a massive coronary three weeks after turning fifty-three. I did have just cause to be concerned about my hypertension. I was determined not to take any medication. I did not take the option of taking time off and resuming later. I had neither the extra time nor money. If I got hurt, I would just have to deal with the consequences.

As each week passed, getting closer to graduation, both the pain in my hands and blood pressure intensified, yet the patients kept coming. I was just happy the quality of my work was still good and patients were appreciative and left feeling better. I counted down the weeks as well as the increases in blood pressure. I was asymptomatic, but I had relatives that were incapacitated by and/or died from sudden strokes due to their hypertension.

Graduation came at last (not too soon). I was fortunate enough to have graduated with the highest GPA and greatest number of patients treated in the clinic (for my class). The clinic director asked me to stay on until others would join in the clinic because the next class due in the clinic was smaller than normal. My director did not ever know the problems I was dealing with. I figured since she was an African American female who was director of our naprapathic clinic that she had "problems" of her own. I had a great respect for her energy, compassion, and positive attitude.

In spite of my pain (which she never knew), I said yes. I promised I would stay until her birthday on March 15, 2012. (She asked me early November 2011.) Her birthday was so ironic. It was the birthday of my children's mother. I have had so many ironies in my life. I feel things were guided by a higher power, or at least I was brainwashed to believe that. Either way, I felt God would take care of me. The clinic director was also a person of faith, so it made it easier to commit to the extra time I spent in the clinic.

I did have to take a break to get away for a while. I went on a trip to Brazil with a group of other healthcare workers and members of People to People International, a humanitarian group started by the former president Dwight D. Eisenhower to promote humanitarian issues and increase our knowledge of each other across the globe. It felt great to get a much-deserved break from the clinic for a week or so. We first flew into São Paulo for a few days. We interacted with local officials, and in our downtime toured various locations like the prestigious art museum in São Paulo. On the streets of São Paulo, we saw some of the most beautiful and creative Christmas decorations. I had no doubts that this country had the largest Catholic population in the world. There was also an opportunity to try a popular local drink called a caipirinha, which was introduced to Brazil, ironically, through its slave population (a slavery that would last until 1890).

After seeing the sites and having a taste of Brazillian cuisine, we flew to Rio De Janeiro the next day. We were going to spend a few more days visiting emergency personnel and seeing how they responded to natural disasters and other catastrophes. We would also visit the sites (i.e., Christ the Redeemer, Tijuca National Forest), and we were invited to visit a favela to see the positive things that people are doing for themselves. Our group went to this bar that was influenced by the "Girl from Ipanema" (a popular song in the 1960s).

On our first day there, I had to walk on the beach barefoot and feel the warm sand on my feet and let the cool refreshing waters of the South Atlantic wash over my feet. I realized now I had visited my fifth continent and touched my fifth ocean. I remember taking a cable car up to a place called Sugar Loaf Mountain which had such an amazing view of Rio that I thought I was in a postcard. It literally took my breath away. I wondered if heaven was this beautiful. The experience was enhanced by more caipirinhas at the café area where rich Brazilian food was also served. The café was so scenic with a great view of Rio and a nice evening breeze coming in from the South Atlantic Ocean.

Rio was as beautiful as they say it was, as well as its people. They looked somewhere between black and white, which made sense not only because of its former slave history but also because of the influx of Portuguese, Italians, and other Mediterranean countries. There were also Afro-Brazilians. The country has the largest number of people of African descent outside of Africa, even more so than the United States.

What a colorful people in Rio, a rainbow of humanity and classes. I saw indigenous people before slavery was introduced. I saw people of African descent. I saw people of Asian descent. I saw people of European descent and various mixtures of the aforementioned. What a collection, a great palette of the creator.

I remember visiting the favela. We had escorts with walkie-talkies to communicate our whereabouts and movements. We visited some of their fledgling entrepreneurial ventures into the arts: a state-of-the-art recording studio, a dance studio, an indoor theater, and an outdoor theater. We witnessed a few performances and definitely bought our share of items produced there onsite—music, videos, T-shirts, etc. We wanted to help support the programming here.

As a black man from America, it gave me a sense of humility and happiness for these people who endured slavery and racism more than we have in the States. The entrepreneurial spirit here amongst those of African descent that I witnessed was just as strong as my people in the states. Since I was the only African American male in our group, I noticed a lot of pictures being taken of me at the favela, where there is a great number of Brazilians of African ancestry.

When we left, I felt encouraged. I remember President Obama's words "Yes, we can," or here it would be "Si se puede" (although that is Spanish and not Portuguese, which is what is spoken in Brazil). Portuguese seems like such a soft and smooth language. Its quality reminded me a lot of French in how it was spoken—very classy and elegant.

The next day, we would visit Tijuca National Forest with its beautiful wildlife, and we would take the majestic trip to visit the statue of Christ the Redeemer atop the mountain. It was awesome and breathtaking. The figure of Christ amidst the clouds gave it a heavenly feel (as if I've ever been to heaven). This place was so surreal. I saw different people from across the globe. Looking at this statue of Christ with his welcoming, outstretched arms looking out over Rio De Janiero, I wondered about the immigrants that came to my country looking at the Statue of Liberty and its welcoming countenance. I believe I got a good shot of the statue with my camera/cell phone.

On our descent, we found a nice place to eat lunch. What a view we had of Rio. We definitely witnessed some grand areas, but being from

Englewood in Chicago, I could appreciate the poverty as well, especially when those in poverty looked like me.

The day we left we had beautiful weather. One of my closest friends collected sand from the local beach. We had seafood pizza that I treated everyone to. This place was in front of the hotel, right by the beach. It was always busy, serving Brazilian delicacies. We ate well. I also had a bottle of cachaça, which is the liquor of the sugarcane that the slaves used to make the first caipirinhas. We were fortunate enough to be provided a room until our bus came to pick us up to go to the airport. Everyone brought something to the table. One person brought a coconut that was purchased on the beach (for juice). Another person brought lime juice purchased from a local market. Another person got us ice. Another person provided snacks, and so on. Here we were, this multiethnic, multi-raced group of Americans following our own Brazilian model. We had our own party before leaving this beautiful yet still in development paradise/nation. Next stop: Chicago.

I returned to the clinic reenergized with about three months to go. My hands appreciated the rest although the pain did not go away. It was now 2012—I would be fifty this year. My youngest son, Brandon, would graduate from college. I was so psyched up to visit my uncle Lonnie for his ninety-fifth birthday and my fiftieth birthday. He was such an entrepreneur, self-starter, and businessman—me, not so much. I definitely had my accomplishments. It's just that business and being an entrepreneur was not in my gift bag at birth. Maybe I will develop that later.

I finished up clinic in mid-March as promised. I finished not too soon. I felt as if my hands were going to fall off. I did not want to manipulate the back. I did not like the feeling of compression on my hands. The pressure of forcefully pushing down became a problem for me. I figured if I could modify what I learned as a naprapath (to stay within my scope of practice), physical therapist assistant, massage therapist, tuina practitioner, and Thai massage practitioner, I would have a combination that worked for my body as well as the clients/patients. I would still be able to promote wellness and at the same time provide manual therapy (my passion). I experimented (and continue to do so) every day. This action has been helpful in me prolonging my manual therapy/massage career.

Massage therapy has always been my first love (for over twenty years). It is a shame massage does not get its just due. I guess it was due to the negative portrayals in some media outlets and the antiquated, stereotyped, and sexualized view of massage therapy and massage therapists in general. It is an uphill climb. So many people grow up with such a conflicted view of touch and the appropriateness and inappropriateness of it. The answer lies in educating the public and our growing utilization by other healthcare providers like medical doctors, osteopaths, chiropractors, physical therapists, etc. The more professional we act, the more professional we will be treated.

It was so sad my uncle did not make it to his ninety-fifth birthday. His death marked the last of the elders I grew up with. It was the end of an era for me as well as Covington, Tennessee, to lose one of its pioneers in black-owned business as well as bridging the race gap with his great barbecue. He had family as well as two white men as pallbearers. I was honored to be a pallbearer to such a great man.

Going back home from Tennessee, I was glad I was going to do something this year to celebrate my fiftieth year on this planet—something monumental. I was going to Antarctica. Since my uncle and others in the family had been groundbreakers, innovators, and pioneers, I wanted to do something that no one had done in my family. Since travel was my forte, I decided I would go to a place few black men had gone to. Since I had already been north of the Arctic Circle and underneath the water as a submariner, going to Antarctica seemed like a logical choice. I had taken care of all the necessary paperwork and the projected day of departure was in December. I was so excited—my sixth continent and sixth ocean (Southern Ocean).

I went back to my old routine of just working three jobs. I worked at the chiropractor on Mondays, at the spa for six days including Mondays, and a forty-hour week at the Home for the Developmentally Disabled at night. My days were full, but I was definitely focused on the upcoming trip.

My fiftieth birthday came and went, but my focus was getting information to prepare for my expedition to Antarctica, as well as my trip to see my son Brandon graduate from Western Washington University. What a fiftieth year this would be.

I purchased my gear for Antarctica at Uncle Dan's in Evanston and K-mart. I made sure I had thermal wear from head to foot. I read about the Antarctic Peninsula (where we would be going) as well as questioned my travel agent. She offered me people I could communicate with who had gone to Antarctica before, but I wanted to be surprised. I wanted to be overwhelmed.

People asked, "Why are you going there?" I replied, "Why not?" which is my name backwards (Y not). I believe the world belongs to all its people, therefore I was exercising my right of freedom of movement. This was my equivalent to drinking out of the white water fountain. This was my equivalent to sitting in the front of the bus. This trip was not just for me, but for anyone who wanted to go past a restricted boundary. It did not matter whether it was physical, mental, class, racial/ethnic, religious, or sexual boundaries. Antarctica would be my Selma, although the only beating I took was to my bank account.

To my chagrin and amazement, I was the only black man or person of Black African ancestry in the expedition. The reason I put it like this is because there was one white South African couple. (They were very polite and friendly.) Her husband was on the expedition to take pictures freelance, so I guess it was a working vacation. There were others there from Great Britain and Scandinavia who were also there for creative reasons, such as taking pictures of various birds, or seals, or whales, or terrain. There were a number of people in their sixties and older for whom this trip was the trip of a lifetime. I could feel their excitement. I already had my own. There were a great number of English, German, Norwegian and Dutch onboard. There were a few South Americans, Canadians and a sprinkle of other people as far away as China, New Zealand, and India. What a cosmopolitan cast.

We hit at least five or six points on the Antarctic Peninsula. We used Polarcirkel boats from the ship to land on shore. I have never seen so many penguins before in my life. We were fortunate to have sun every day. Since we were below the equator and this was December, we were in the end of Antarctica's spring. The sun was very bright, bright enough for me to get sunburnt (the first time in my life), which was annoying and painful. I now know how some white people feel.

For every meal, I tried to sit with someone different from a different country. I was curious about lifestyles in different countries. Everyone seemed open for conversation. We always had just one seating since there were only around 120 of us. I felt as if we were in a class or on an expedition (which I guess we were).

In transit across the Drake Passage into the Southern Ocean (which surrounds Antarctica), there were numerous lectures on the wildlife in the region, the geology, and the geopolitics of Antarctica, and all the different claims to different areas of Antarctica by other countries. I was thoroughly fascinated at each landing point. The ship would remain a distance from shore, and we would go to and from via the Polarcirkel boats to land. What an exhilarating experience to feel the cold Antarctic air with a slight spritz on the face. Having grown up in Chicago, this weather wasn't too bad.

After a few more days of landings and looking at various seals, penguins, whales, and other sea life and birds, it was time to return to Ushuaia, Argentina, the furthest city south in the world. We visited a national forest, ate lunch, and saw some of the fantastic terrain and wildlife. Antarctica was over, but the memories will last a lifetime. I felt like I was in a postcard. It was so pristine—no pollution, no smog, not even the tiniest scrap of litter. The mantra of our guides was "Take nothing but photographs; leave nothing but footprints"—which we did.

There was a charter flight we took from Ushuaia to Buenos Aires. In Buenos Aires, we spent the night at this grand hotel, but first we experienced a tango show—what a sight. What skill, grace, poise, excitement. What a trip. The next morning came too soon, but there was a final river boat tour of Rio de la Plata and the beautiful homes and boats that dotted the landscape. I did not know if I would go back home. My son was graduating in a few days, so I had something new and worthwhile to focus on.

The trip from Buenos Aires to Chicago was uneventful, but I did get a chance to visit Eva Perón's gravesite. What a woman.

Back in the States, I was so excited about my son's college graduation. He had already accepted a job offer in Portland at a place he had an internship just that past summer. I was so happy for him. He graduated with honors and secured a job in his field of study in this tight economy—what an accomplishment. I went out to dinner after the graduation with my sons Brandon and Brian, their mom Cynthia, and her husband Mark. I felt so blessed to see all my children as adults working and doing their own thing. My daughter, Brianna, could not come because she was in the military (U.S. Navy) on the East Coast. I believe she saw the graduation online.

After dinner, Brandon went out with his friends. I gave him the complimentary jacket I received when I went to Antarctica. My eldest son Brian and I walked around Seattle's downtown area. I saw a statue of Jimi Hendrix I had never seen before. We saw a movie. We also just walked and talked. We spent the night at a local place he had been to before. We had breakfast at another local funky (in a good way) type of place. The food was great. I was enjoying this time with my son, but it was also somber, because I knew it would soon be over. After a hearty breakfast and even heartier laughter, I dropped my son off in Downtown Seattle and headed toward the airport.

What a great December. What a way to end my fiftieth year on this planet. I wondered what was to be in 2013?

Chapter Eleven

I wanted to complete all seven continents and all seven oceans. I wanted to go to Australia next and let the waters of the South Pacific run over my feet. I contacted my travel agent, who was also was a client (how convenient). She ran some dates by me. The date in August worked out perfect for me.

I wanted to have seen all seven continents and seven oceans while I was still fifty. My goal was now going to become a reality. I really felt the Lord on my side with this. I was getting more clients, so I could save more.

I received some alarming news in late January when I took my routine physical for one of my jobs. This physical happened to include blood work (since I was fifty). I found out two disturbing things: one, my blood pressure was higher than when I was in the naprapathic clinic, and two, my cholesterol was significantly over two hundred. My MD (who was a graduate of Northwestern University) was giving me recommendations for different types of drugs/medications and was asking me which drugstore would be the most convenient to send my medication to. I thought, *I had this great education as a naprapath, and I had three semesters of nutrition; let me see if I could turn this around myself before I got on the medication rollercoaster.* I told my doctor to give me three months to turn things around. I thought of that old adage, "Physician, heal thyself."

It was time for me to "get busy." For the next six weeks, I would eat oatmeal for breakfast (to decrease cholesterol). I would add almonds or walnuts to increase protein. I would have a green drink during the day for additional vitamins, minerals, and fiber. I would have a salad with rice and beans for dinner. Over the next ninety days, I also took the following supplements: red yeast rice (for cholesterol), Lecithin (for cholesterol) odorless garlic (for cardiovascular function), a male multivitamin (for my overall health), Cal-Mag-Zinc (calcium, magnesium, and zinc, for bones, muscles, antioxidants, and blood pressure), DHA (for cardiovascular function), DHEA (for continued testosterone production), green tea (to assist with cardiovascular function), Chromium Picolinate (to even out blood sugar), B Complex as well as B-12 (for energy/metabolism), milk thistle (for kidney/liver purification,) and L-Arginine, hawthorn berry, and celery supplements (for high blood pressure).

It sounds like a lot, but I was determined not to go on medications. My mom had been on medications from the time of my brother's birth (when she was thirty) to the time of her death (at fifty-three). She also had a tremendous amount of pressure/stress on her, especially after my dad's death and from financial issues. I realized I had to change the situation. My grandmother (Mom's mom) had hypertension, although she died of cancer in her early seventies. I remember my uncle Wilbert, who I got my genealogical information from, had hypertension, and would later die from a stroke relatively early in his retirement—and he was an award winning athlete.

I found out working the third shift did not help. I could not change shifts right now. I had to find a solution to this problem.

I read labels like a hawk—anything with sodium, especially soda, did not make the shopping cart. To the best of my ability, I eliminated processed food. I had fish instead of meat. I was losing weight as well. I went from 175 to 165 in a few weeks. I was feeling better as well. There were no more bloodshot eyes. I was more alert and less tired during the night shift. I had greater energy (I felt). It seemed I accomplished more.

About halfway through (six weeks later), I had to check to see how I was doing. My blood pressure was 120/80, and this was after my night shift. My cholesterol had dropped into the 170s; my doctor was very impressed. He said he knew of no one who had turned things around so quickly (especially in the African American community) without the use of some medication. The nutritional changes worked for me. Applying what I learned helped me reduce my high cholesterol and high blood pressure. Those factors alone were worth the money to become a naprapath. I wish my mother, grandmother, aunt, uncle, and all my other relatives that had passed on had known what I knew. I don't know if they would have complied with the necessary dietary changes.

By the ninetieth day, mark my blood pressure was 115/75, and my cholesterol was 155. My physician asked me even more questions this time. I had started to eat meat again but sparingly—chicken once a week and beef once a month. My numbers were still good. I believe if I would have gone totally vegan, my numbers would have been lower, but my weight had dropped to 160, so I felt I was losing too much lean muscle mass. I felt if I was judicious about the meat (mostly chicken and fish) and how it was prepared (nothing fried, mostly baked or roasted), I would be fine.

I received a text from my daughter early in the year about a cousin I knew nothing about (Jimmie N. Bethel) on the Internet who was looking for other Bethels (I believe through Ancestry.com). My daughter was much more tech-savvy and social media-savvy than I. I asked her to send me a copy in the mail, and I would make sure all the relatives I knew would get it.

When I received the document, it was an invitation to a family reunion to be held in Burlington, North Carolina—in Alamance County, where the American side of the family began. The reunion would be in June. When I received the document, I believe it was late March/early April, so there was still time. I sent copies to all the Bethels I knew. My daughter gave me Cousin Jimmie's phone number, and we talked like old friends. He was my great-uncle Oscar's great-grandson. How ironic. I am Charles Henry Bethel's great-grandson (Oscar's younger brother).

It was a pleasant coincidence to get a clean bill of health before the reunion in June. The reunion would also be about two months before my trip to Australia in August. All this fun before turning fifty-one.

Jimmy and I talked a few more times before I attended the reunion in Burlington, North Carolina—in Alamance County. The people who were able to go from the copies I sent out were my elder brother Sam (our patriarch), my eldest sister Dana, and my elder sister Dee. We were all born two years apart—Dana, Sam, Dee, and I. My cousin Wanda and her daughter Shavonne would be in attendance. I was so excited. Finally, the Bethels would be together in North Carolina after all these years—our homecoming in 2013, 150 years after the Emancipation Proclamation. I truly felt free. What a family history. What a journey for all our members. I wondered what states would be represented. I wondered about the stories being told. I was beside myself with anticipation.

I also made arrangements for my little brother's son Teddy to go. He was now going into high school, which meant more football and a whole new world academically. Teddy and I had just visited my sons in Portland, Oregon to celebrate Father's Day. I was sad that my own sons would not be there due to work commitments, but I understood.

The day of travel came. It was a very rainy night in North Carolina (typical for this time of year, I was told). We arrived in Raleigh-Durham to meet my sister Dee, who was waiting for us. She arrived from Denver a bit before us. She purchased a rental car for the three of us. Burlington was not too far to the west.

We sadly found out the plane my other siblings was on was diverted to Detroit. I was at a loss for words. The weather system was just that bad. The earliest flight would put them in Raleigh-Durham after the time of the reunion. I was so disappointed. We would not all be there at the first reunion in North Carolina—where it all began.

Dee drove us through the dark and rainy night on the interstate through the lush forests of North Carolina, trying to avoid the deer out that night. I was thinking how I was going home to where it all started—well, almost. Alamance County is the same county that my distant cousin Alex Haley's relatives (and mine) left in a wagon train going from Alamance County to Lauderdale County in West Tennessee. My relatives settled in Tipton County (which is just south of Lauderdale County). Both counties have the Mississippi River as a western border. This was the new frontier post–slavery—for some. I felt like I had a connection with this area, and I thought of Nidra, her daughter Caroline, and her grandson Charles Henry. All of them lived around this area, but Nidra was originally from West Africa.

We pulled into Burlington after midnight. Dee, Teddy, and I got our rooms and had a good sleep. The morning came soon enough. We had breakfast. It was complimentary with our stay. The food was Southern style (there goes my diet). There were eggs, bacon, sausage, grits, and biscuits and gravy. It was all made with that typical Southern flair. It was all good. I would fast/detox when I got home. Now was a time for celebration.

To see the different family resemblances and nuances in behavior was fascinating. It was great to see my cousin Jimmie and his family (wife Angela, son Nigel, and daughter Noelle). It was funny and interesting to notice my cousin's build—short, stocky, and that Bethel smile. Bethel men typically were short and stocky, although my father was six feet tall", my brother Ted was five feet eleven, and little Teddy and myself were five feet ten.

Teddy, Dee, and I loved seeing our newfound relatives. I only wished my sister Dana and brother Sam could have made it for this momentous occasion. Cousin Jimmie was an expert at multimedia equipment. We watched this excellent video containing family members and some of the family history. The discs were available to purchase (the proceeds going to a fund for future reunions). The intermingling of white and black in our family started when young Nidra, who came here as a child from West Africa, reached early womanhood. To the best of my knowledge, there was just one child with the owner of the plantation: William Bethell, Jr. (who was originally from Caswell County, North Carolina). The white Bethells seemed to have two Ls at the end of their names, while the black Bethels had just one L. I don't know if this was forced or just done to distinguish one side from the other. I knew there were white Bethels (possibly no relation) who lived in the United Kingdom, United States, Ireland, and the Caribbean Islands (traced with Ancestry.com and FamilyTreeDNA.com).

The banquet was so much fun. It was there where Teddy, Dee, and I met up with cousin Wanda and her daughter Shavonne. Their flight came in via Greensboro, North Carolina. We all sat at the same table. We discussed how life was going. We found out about something which was rumored about but now confirmed—that Caroline and Samuel Bethell (who were half brother and sister) had three children together (Ollie Minta, Oscar, and Charles Henry). It was one of those negative facts of slavery—in a number of cases (truth be told), the slaves' and owners' blood were blended. These people owned their own relatives. I then thought of Thomas Jefferson and Sally Hemings; although not related by blood, it is believed they had six children together, and it is a possibility that Sally Hemings was the half-sister of Jefferson's wife. I also thought about the activist and TV personality Al Sharpton being distantly related to Strom Thurmond, the Dixiecrat, as well as how Thurmond himself fathered an African American, Essie Mae Washington-Williams.

I know I could find enough anomalies to make another book. We are all Americans, but sharing genes does not necessarily mean sharing ideals. I wondered about this thing called "blackness". How much is genetics? How much is in your heart? Who is "blacker": Clarence Thomas or Eminem? Does it even matter? Is it socialized? Do you walk your talk? How much do you compromise? When is too much too much? And when you compromise to survive, are you surviving?

I was so pleased at the youth I saw at the reunion, especially the young males. They countered all the stereotypes. They were well-mannered, church-going, respected in their communities, and college-bound. The young ladies were the same. I was uplifted, but then I thought of families that were not so lucky like Trayvon Martin, Oscar Grant, and Michael Brown. Coast-to-coast it seems like black male youths are being targeted. I was happy that my family was together here in North Carolina, safe and secure, enjoying each other's company, trading stories about our lives and our families. We were bonding and getting a feeling of solidarity.

Sunday came soon enough and we had church, a rousing sermon, and then a great meal at a local place where there was trading of addresses and phone numbers. Dee, Teddy, and I then left for the airport. She would be going back to Denver, we to Chicago. I was saddened that my other siblings flew back to Denver from Detroit, although they would have missed a great deal of the celebration if they would have waited for a connecting flight.

The past weekend left me with a lot to think about in terms of blackness and whiteness and what it truly means to be family. Caroline and her children were raised in the "big house." The children of Caroline and Samuel (Ollie Minta, Oscar, and Charles Henry) attended lessons with the other white children—their half-siblings in the household (from what I was told). In fact, my great-grandfather was the favorite, and he was quite intelligent. I also wondered if it was because of his Nordic appearance (see the cover of the book) more than his quick mind.

My great-uncle Oscar (my cousin Jimmie's great–grandfather) was quite the businessman/dealer. He was able to talk his white half-brother out of a horse for himself. Due to my great-uncle's appearance and how his behavior was accepted and tolerated, he actually thought he was white until at the age of sixteen, when he was told he was a slave. Needless to say, he did not take it well.

This whole concept of blackness and whiteness fascinates me. I wonder why it exists even when there is substantial scientific evidence pointing to the fact that we can all trace our origins back to Africa. There is just one race: the human race. I wondered what all three primary colors of human beings would look like (Asian, black, white). My guess would be Filipino since all three cultures have been represented in their history. Many people in the Philippines have Spanish-sounding names due to that country's influence in their culture. The original islanders were black; the Europeans referred to them as Negritos. I then wondered about Australia and its original people, who some call Aborigines but who prefer the term Blackfellas.

August was here before I knew it, and I was going to Australia. I took Qantas out of O'Hare in Chicago to Dallas and from Dallas to Sydney via Brisbane. On the flight, I saw two great Australian movies. The first was *Australia* with Hugh Jackman and Nicole Kidman. The movie increased my empathy for the Blackfellas of Australia and a reminder of the treatment of dark versus light on all six of the inhabited continents. I was coming from a country that had elected a black person as the president of (arguably) the most powerful nation on Earth, and I was watching these two great movies (*Australia* and *The Sapphires*) to a certain extent mimic American history.

I was excited to complete my "world traveler" status. The trip was not only important to me but to all the blacks (worldwide) who could not go where they wanted to because of the color of their skin. I believe this planet belongs to all of us. As a representative of one of the first people of the planet, I was honored and humbled to make this trip.

The Aussies that I met were polite, engaging, unguarded, and friendly. I ate New Zealand lamb at a place called the Quay (pierside). I visited Manly Beach via ferry. I walked along the beach and let the South Pacific wash over my dress shoes (just a little). Mission complete.

I am sure other black men have traveled the seven continents and seen the seven oceans. I know other black men that have doctorates. I know other black men that were officers in the U.S. Military. I am sure there are black men that have completed five marathons. I know other black men that have made (and in my case, lost) a million dollars. But I am the only one I know of who came from Englewood. I have done all these things for my race. I am tired, but my color still pushes me. As long as I am black, it will never be enough.

I realize at this point looking out over the vast South Pacific that there is but one race: the human race. I have been trying to prove myself my entire life. The circuit is complete. It stops here! If society does not believe I am accomplished now, that is society's fault.

From this point forward, my allegiance is to God and myself—a God who has no color. For Jews, Christians, and Muslims, we are all able to trace our earthly father to Abraham, so from now on, that will be my belief. I am a child of Abraham who practices Christianity, no greater or lesser than my Jewish and Muslim brothers and sisters. I see them also as children of Abraham—their religion is secondary. I feel as if a weight has been lifted and I have transcended. Sure, outwardly I am still black (and will always be). In addition to that, though, I am a citizen of the Earth, a child of Abraham, residing in the United States.

Manly Beach got its name (rumor has it) from the manly bearing of the Blackfellas that were once more abundant than they are now and roamed more "freely" throughout the Australian Continent. I also thought about the second Australian movie I saw, *The Sapphires*, where one of the characters was mixed between black and white and how she bravely navigated to finally just be herself, which brought her greatest success.

After visiting Manly Beach, I went back to the ferry. The view of the Sydney Opera House was so stunning in the afternoon sun I had to find out if any shows were on for that evening. To my surprise and amazement there was—it was the jazz artist George Benson. God was smiling on me. I purchased a ticket for that evening's performance.

I had to see one more thing before the concert: the Sydney Tower. I opted to pay the additional fee to walk outside at the uppermost level of the tower (with a guide and safety net of course). The people in my group were from all over the world: South America, Eastern Europe, India, and our guide was a mixture of Kiwi (New Zealander) and Pacific Islander. He looked a lot like one of my mixed cousins back in the States. He was very knowledgeable, friendly, and safe, and he made sure we followed all the safety precautions. The view was majestic and fantastic.

It was getting near evening and Sydney was lighting up. The Sydney Bridge was well lit, like an ornament. The lights on the tower itself were brilliant, highlighting its red logo. We could see the mountains to the south and the hustling bustling Quay (pierside). All seemed complete. I traveled land, sea, and air in Australia all in a matter of hours.

I still had a George Benson concert I had to get to. I walked from the Sydney Tower to the Opera House for the great evening view. It's funny how lighting can change a scene. The Opera House looked even more magnificent at night highlighted by the additional lighting. I was thinking what a great reward George Benson was. This was the gravy, the cherry on top of my seventh continent and seventh ocean quest. George Benson would only be here for two nights, and this was the first night—how lucky/blessed I was! I honestly believe God was telling me that this was all meant to be.

I did not see too many people in the audience that looked like me, but the environment was upbeat and positive. When Mr. Benson played "Give Me Night," the whole audience was on their feet dancing, from the balcony to the main floor. Some people were even dancing in the aisles. It was a great sight to see, all of us dancing and no one caring, just enjoying each other's company for this moment in time. George Benson sung all his old standards and did a tribute to one of my other jazz heroes, Nat King Cole, who grew up in Chicago, Illinois—my hometown. The Lord was definitely talking to me. I felt so blessed.

After the concert, I took a cab to my hotel by the airport. My cabbie was an Aussie who asked me about my travels. When I told him Australia was my seventh continent, he was impressed and pleased. When I got to my hotel room, the first thing I did was get down on my knees by the bed and thanked God. I wept. I know this was not Selma or Montgomery, and it was not Cicero or Chicago, but in a small way (my own way) it was my contribution to tearing down barriers: meeting people, talking with them in intelligent conversation, dispelling myths and stereotypes. I felt my travels and interacting with other people in the world was one less hurdle for a black man. In order for me to know the world, I must also be willing to let the world know me and reach out (in spite of the past).

The next day I left, on the long flight back to the United States. I met an African American man who had his own business. He had been in Auckland, New Zealand on a business trip and had a break in Sydney yesterday. We traded stories, and he saw some of the sites I did not. I felt relieved to see other people like me traveling, making their mark on the world. It gave me hope for the world as a whole and my community in particular.

It felt so odd to get back into Dallas time-wise (almost the same time we had left Sydney on the same day). I also left Sydney to similar weather in Dallas. It felt like a sci-fi movie, being transported in time from one place to another in twenty-four hours, yet the time on your clock moved only a few minutes. It also reminded me of when we dream and the whole dissolution of the time and space concept, like going through years in our dreams when we sleep, only to wake up a few hours later.

I landed in Dallas a new person.

Chapter Twelve

All the life goals I had set I had attained. What next? First, I thanked God. I then went back on my diet of oatmeal for breakfast and salad for dinner. My oatmeal was from McDonald's, and I had a veggie Cantina Bowl from Taco Bell. It had helped me this far with my blood pressure and cholesterol readings. Since I worked three jobs, I had a limited amount of time for food preparation. I had a major physical in September that I was preparing for. A traveling group called Life Line Screening® would be in the Lombard area, so I decided to take advantage of this opportunity. I wanted to start the next fifty years off right. I was having a good time trying to get ready for my physical exam. I was now fifty-one.

The test day came. It was the moment of truth. I was poked and prodded. I had some routine blood work. My blood pressure was taken (115/75). It wasn't bad. It was my lowest recorded score. My cholesterol would come back as 155, also my lowest recorded score. There were no problems with bone density, abdominal aneurisms, potential blockages, or risks of stroke. This would be a great way to end the year, since so many of my relatives have had hypertension or strokes. I felt nothing could stop me—until the phone call from my daughter in the military.

I wondered what was wrong. Brianna had come back from the Middle East for a while now. She and her husband Mike had been married for a while now. He was in the Marines and had completed a tour in Afghanistan. He was now out of the military and going to school. My daughter informed me of her miscarriage. I was disappointed of course, but I wanted to say something positive. I told her, "It will happen in God's time—I am sure of it". My daughter, being a Christian, agreed and sounded more upbeat. It lifted me up to hear her positive-sounding voice. For a father who had not always been around, any kind word from her (or any of my children) was greatly treasured.

I connected with all my children in different ways. For my daughter and I, it was about empathy, feelings, and duty to a certain extent. She was the only child to follow in my foot steps to join the military (U.S. Navy). She was at Great Lakes, Illinois, as I had been. I witnessed her boot camp graduation about twenty-five years after I had been there. Life had come full circle, and I was almost a grandpa. I figured all things will happen in good time, and the Lord knows best (as always).

The rest of 2013 was somber and filled with much work and routine day-to-day stuff. I was still on my diet, exercising, and using weights two to three times a week. My weight had gone from the upper 170s down to the upper 160s. I felt lighter. My clothes were looser yet more comfortable.

I had my work physical in late January/early February. My MD (and Northwestern graduate) who was normally very stoic in appearance, was animated. He wanted to know exactly what I did to get my cholesterol down. Full disclosure, my cholesterol was in the mid-170s (up from September) but I did splurge some from Halloween to New Year's Day, and my blood pressure was 120/80. My doctor wanted to know what worked for me, so I told him.

I had breakfast at McDonald's (oatmeal and a container of orange juice) and sometimes a cup of coffee. I would buy a green naked juice to have something to take my supplements with and increase my minerals. I had a men's multivitamin and a calcium, magnesium, and zinc supplement to help decrease muscle tension and to help decrease blood pressure. I had red yeast rice to decrease cholesterol (for the first year). I also used Lecithin to decrease cholesterol and help nerve tissue. I used hawthorn berry to decrease blood pressure. I also used celery seed to decrease blood pressure. I used garlic for overall health, but especially the cardiovascular system. I used Turmeric, Bromelain, and Ginger as anti-inflammatories. I used L-Arginine for Blood Pressure. I used COQ-10 for the heart as well as L-Carnitine. I used milk thistle to detoxify the liver, Glucosamine and Chondroitin for my joints, Chromium Picolinate to balance blood sugar, B Complex/B12 to help with energy/metabolism, Asian Ginseng for energy, DHEA to counter aging of the cells, and fish oil for the cardiovascular system and to fight inflammation. I would have naked green juice and raw almonds throughout the day to snack on. For dinner, I would have a veggie Cantina Bowl from Taco Bell or a salad from a local Mediterranean place. I believe since our red blood cells live about 120 days (four months), a person could try three diets a year if they wanted to find the right diet for themselves and tweak it according to their blood tests (vitally important) and other vitals like blood pressure and heart rate.

Energy level and quality of life are so important. If a person is totally relying on taste or if they have financial issues that do not allow them to purchase the supplements (like I experienced with my patients in the clinic), it is still possible to be healthy even if the turnaround time would be greater. I am thinking about certain spices/herbs like turmeric, ginger, and garlic. Eating sardines or salmon (two or three times a week depending on your budget) can be done for your fish oils. You can also eat fresh pineapple for bromelain and fresh papaya for papain to help with digestion and decrease inflammation. Hopefully most adults could afford a once-a-day multivitamin. I would also say to decrease all processed and fast food. Also, you could make healthier choices like oatmeal or salads or vegetable selections. Fruits without additional sauces/creams or sodium and sugars are also good. I can only say these items worked for me. If it is a placebo effect (which I doubt), it has kept my cholesterol in the 170s or lower and maintains my blood pressure at 120/80, and I still have a high energy level. Water is the beverage of choice (a must).

My MD was impressed. He told me he had not seen anyone turn their cholesterol around as quickly as I had, especially without medications. He lamented to me about people's compliance with dietary changes (which I was all too familiar with) in our African American community.

I also thought of people with pre-existing conditions. Two former mentors/teachers came to mind. They both have passed on. They both had cardiovascular problems. Both were naprapaths—one black, one white. Both were in their fifties (as I now am). I think of my own mother who I had to remove from life support (who had just turned fifty-three the month before) after a massive heart attack. I am also reminded of stars like Barry White and Luther Vandross who both died of cardiovascular problems in their fifties. The threat is real, especially to the African American community.

Having passed my work physical, I was looking forward to the next Bethel family reunion in late June in Charlotte, North Carolina.

My cousin Jimmie Bethel had told me that the first reunion last June had been so successful that other relatives wanted to come. We had eighty-eight people in Burlington the year before. We were possibly anticipating more than two hundred this year—I was hopeful.

Work continued to flourish. I was happy with the overall reviews of Simply Beautiful in Lombard, Illinois. I was particularly pleased with my reviews on Yelp pertaining to my massage services and the LinkedIn connections I have made (people from six continents and fifty states). I felt blessed. It can be so difficult for a male in this field of work, yet this could also be seen as a challenge to overcome (which is how I've seen it for twenty years now). The extra money earned would come in handy for the Father's Day trip I would be taking to Portland, Oregon to see my sons, as well as for the Bethel family reunion in Charlotte, North Carolina a couple of weeks later.

In early spring, I heard from my daughter again. I was hoping for some positive news, since I have always associated spring with a fresh start and hope. It has the Resurrection as well as Passover—a new start. Her voice was calm, but I could tell she was holding back something. I was hoping and praying that the news would be positive. We exchanged greetings. I did not want to seem too anxious because I did not want to pressure her. Then she said slowly and plainly, "I'm pregnant."

I could now breathe. I could now be happy. I could now be a grandfather. I wanted to know the details. How long has she been pregnant? What names are being thought of? Why did she wait so long to tell me? I was so happy for her and Mike. I also mentioned about the family reunion and when it was to occur in late June. From what she told me, I was estimating she would be in her late fifth or early sixth month at this time. I figured there was no way she was going to make it, although she could have since Virginia borders North Carolina. Either way, I did not want to pressure her. I said nonchalantly that I was going to the reunion.

I later found out that both of my sisters, my older brother, and his daughter (my niece Alisha) would be going. My cousin Wanda and her sister Debbie and Wanda's two (of four) adult children, Kristen and John, would also be attending. Teddy's mom gave me permission to take Teddy with me. I was overwhelmed with joy.

My cousin Michael, who works in state government in Tennessee, told me about a William Bethell who was mayor of Memphis (I believe the fifteenth one) and that he would be a great-uncle. I was not sure how to take this information. William Bethell was white, was probably a Confederate, but was also a family member—or should I just say blood relative, since family usually indicates some type of closeness or acknowledgement. I seriously doubt that this man (even if he were still living) would acknowledge me as his great–nephew, although his white relative, Samuel, would go on to marry Caroline (the mother of his three children: Ollie Minta, Oscar, and Charles Henry, my great-grandfather). I always wondered if it was a marriage of love or convenience. (Not too many owners married their slaves.) All I know is Samuel Bethell must have been a significant influence in his son's life because Charles Henry Bethel named his fourth child Samuel Farnsworth Bethel (note the one L). Ironically, my older brother (my hero growing up) was named Samuel Farnsworth Bethel after our grandfather, not our White great-great-grandfather who our grandfather was named after.

I bet traveling in that wagon train coming from Alamance County, North Carolina to Lauderdale County, Tennessee that my great-grandfather (in his teens) would have a lot of chores and responsibilities. I am blessed that his older sister, Ollie Minta, took him and that her husband Jerry Holt allowed Ollie Minta to bring other family members with her. I am sure this was quite an adventure (depicted in the book *Roots* by my distant cousin, Alex Haley, in Chapter 113, pages 830-832). I think of the useful skill my great-grandfather learned back then—brick masonry—and how he and his cousins (Ollie Minta's sons) James McCadden and George Williamson and others helped build the town of Covington, Tennessee, for both blacks and whites. They built houses and churches and other buildings (like the courthouse featured in the first scene of the movie *A Family Thing* with James Earl Jones and Robert Duvall). There is a street in Covington, Tennessee that bears the family name (Bethel Street). This was to honor my great-grandfather, Charles Henry Bethel, the brick mason who built a number of buildings/churches (one of which, Canaan Baptist Church, is on the National Registry of Historic Places).

What I admire most about my great-grandfather (more than the aforementioned) is the fact that although he could have passed for white and had enough education and skill to distance himself from the African American community, he embraced his heritage. He was an active member of and in the community. I remember not only his legacy, but also my great-grandmother, Callie Bethel, who was his wife. She was a school teacher and a mother to eight of his children. Callie was from Jackson, Tennessee, and lived to be 104 years old. She received a letter of commendation for her longevity from none other than Pres. Jimmy Carter back in the mid-1970s. How fitting to receive this honor from a fellow Southerner (who grew up with blacks in Plains, Georgia) and neighbor (since Georgia borders Tennessee). I see Tennessee as the heart of the South, since it borders eight Southern States: Kentucky, Virginia, North Carolina, Georgia, Alabama, Mississippi, Arkansas, and Missouri. Some would consider Missouri part of the Southwest, but given it was a slave state and its past racial history, I say it is Southern. Ironically, Missouri borders eight states, but not all of them are Southern.

I have always had mixed feelings about the South and its legacy, but it is the place where both my parents were born and raised. It is the place where my siblings and I spent our summers in childhood delight, being spoiled rotten by our kin. Yes, there was the great migration due to racism/lynching and the lack of opportunity. Tennessee was the last Southern State to leave the Union and the first to be accepted back in it. It was the home of Stax and Sun records, the "rock and soul of Memphis, but also of country and bluegrass in Nashville. It was the birth place of the Ku Klux Klan in East Tennessee and the place of the assassination of Dr. Martin Luther King in West Tennessee (Memphis). It was home to Andrew Jackson, a popular president that owned slaves and forcibly moved Native Americans west. It is also home to Al Gore, former popular progressive governor, vice president, and presidential candidate who had a Jewish running mate (Joe Lieberman).

Now look at the progress we have made as a nation to elect our first African American president, Barack Obama. All we have to do now is to let him lead without obstruction.

All in all, I think of Covington, Tennessee, as a second home that I rarely visit.

I went to Portland, Oregon, to see my sons for Father's Day weekend. My son Brandon lives there, and my son Brian came down from Tacoma, Washington. There would be no diets this weekend—just walking, talking, eating, and repeating all of the above. We had a great time catching up.

I did not feel guarded. I was so happy my children were raised near Seattle (Renton) at this time. Now, my son Brandon had this great job in Portland, Oregon. I definitely felt the family as a whole was moving forward, not to mention my siblings in Denver, Colorado, who seemed to be doing well themselves. Maybe there was some truth to Horace Greeley's message, "Go west young man," that applied to us all.

The second reunion was close at hand. I picked up Teddy for our flight to North Carolina. This time, we would be going to Charlotte, the "Queen City." Teddy was taller than me now and filling out rapidly. With his sandy-colored hair and friendly blue eyes, he filled me in on his first year in high school, not only his football exploits but also his exploits in the classroom. This sounded great, considering his many academic struggles in elementary school. He was telling me how he could not wait to have his first car. He had earned his driver's license a few months ago. We talked about his school life and our anticipation to see other relatives, especially since Sam and Dana could not make it last year. The plane could not fly to Charlotte, North Carolina fast enough.

When we got there, we would find Dana via cell phone. We were ecstatic to see her. We had lunch at an airport Wendy's, waiting for my other siblings and niece to arrive. When they arrived (and after many long overdue hugs), we picked up the rental van so we could head out to the hotel. I really wished that Shavonne (Wanda's daughter) could have attended this reunion as well. I also wished my cousins Michael and John from Covington and Memphis, Tennessee could make it. They both had prior job commitments. I fondly remember playing with my cousins and siblings in the hot Tennessee sun. My nephew Tony (my namesake) and my brother Sam's first child (Alisha's brother) also could not make it due to work.

As I was driving from the airport, the van was buzzing with remembrances, old stories, and new stories. All six of us were catching up with each other. Never in my almost thirty-six years of driving have I been so pleasantly distracted. The time between the airport and the hotel seemed nonexistent. I was on a natural high out of this world.

I found out Brianna and her husband Mike would be coming to the reunion. They would be driving from Virginia. God is good. Brianna had not seen her aunts and uncle and cousin Alisha (who was the same age as her) since she was five years old (other than in family pictures). What an adventure to come here.

After checking in and agreeing to meet at a particular point once we all got ready, the race was on. I confirmed with cousin Jimmie where and when we would meet. I thought I was going to have trouble finding out how to get to one place or another since three of the locations were away from the hotel. Modern technology is great, especially in the hands of a young person. What I mean by that statement is how Alisha used Siri from her phone, and I followed her directions to the letter.

When we went to the banquet hall, it was bright and sunny. We met Wanda, Debbie, Kristen, and John there. Other cousins from North Carolina and other states were also present. Some were there from last year's reunion in Burlington, North Carolina. It was so much fun to catch up. We not only seemed like family, but friends as well—no attitudes.

One new arrival was a cousin named Hayward Bethel and his wife, both from Austin, Texas. He was related via George Bethel. Although Caroline was George's mother, Samuel Bethell was not the father. I guess when a person is used for breeding purposes, it would be difficult, if not impossible, to find family decades to one hundred years later, especially if there are geographical differences and no one has kept in touch. Ancestry.com has proven to be quite a useful tool, as well as the work completed by my uncle Dr. Wilbert Jackson, who sent for documents and traveled to various places to help put the genealogy together and kept it in place. Great praise also goes to my cousin Jimmie Bethel for his extensive use of information, especially from Ancestry.com.

We enjoyed heavy "Southern" hors d'oeuvres, with signature sweet tea and lemonade. Cousin Jimmie and his wife Angela were getting a head count to hand out the family T-shirts. We were playing games to familiarize each other with our names and break the ice. This exercise/game required that you talked to other relatives to find out information about them in a non-threatening way. There was a particularly competitive game of musical chairs, in the middle of which Brianna and Michael came in, soaking wet from the recent North Carolina downpour. Brianna seemed in full bloom of her pregnancy. Just to think, at six months, my first grandchild was in there. I was overjoyed. The moment was beautiful and surreal at the same time. Some relatives gathered around Brianna and Mike with questions and conversation.

The musical chair game was still being played out, and the winner had yet to be determined. The game had whittled down to two contestants: my competitive and lively cousin Wanda, and my charming, sly, and witty cousin Hayward. Both were Bethels, but only one could win. It was so entertaining to watch the fake stops and starts, and finally, my cousin Wanda won.

After the competition, we spent more time socializing, catching up, eating, and enjoying the sweet tea, lemonade, and water provided. Brianna, Mike, and I talked for a good while, catching up with each other. They also talked to my siblings and numerous cousins. What a family affair. Although more were supposed to attend, I was so happy we had the fun loving group we had. Everyone was upbeat and positive and happy (genuinely happy) to see one another. We thanked God for this opportunity to reunite us after all those years and being scattered throughout the United States.

The evening eventually came to a close, and we had to go back to our hotel. We all stayed at the same hotel. I drove my siblings, Alisha, and Teddy back. I did not want the night to end. We happened to find a place where we could gather near the lobby—the same place we would be eating breakfast at later that morning. I brought numerous pictures from over the years that showed all our developments over the years from childhood to now, from Charles Henry and Mama Callie to the present. We had fun joking, talking, and teasing each other to the wee hours of the morning. We were just catching up over the lost years. There were thirteen of us present, if you count my grandson Landon in utero (and I did). At some point, we figured out we had to go to sleep so we would have enough energy for the family picnic later that day. The picnic was at a place called Phillip Morris Park, further out from where we would be staying.

The morning of the picnic came soon enough. Breakfast was rich and southern, just as I had remembered. Breakfast was in the same place we lounged in after the first night's celebration. It was fun to see who was an early riser. I was able to catch up with a cousin, James (not Jimmie) Bethel, who had arrived late last night with his two adult sons. They had driven from Maryland through rough rainy weather. We talked for a bit (much too short). Teddy would get up later, but definitely in time for breakfast. It was great to see and converse with my brother Sam, sisters Dana and Dee, and my niece Alisha.

After going to our rooms for a little bit to make final changes, Alisha had "Siri" ready for me, although it was a straight shot from the hotel (for the most part). When we arrived, the other Bethel's from Great-uncle

Oscar's side was there, including cousin Jimmie, his wife Angela, and his son Nigel. Jimmie's youngest, Noelle, would not be in attendance because she was taking part in a special program being offered by her college that summer. She would begin there as a freshman. I remember freshman year. I was so happy for Noelle. Nigel is in a Pre Med program at the same institution as his sister. I am sure cousin Jimmie and Angela felt quite blessed, and they were. I am happy he organized this event to bring us Bethels together. Others arrived at the picnic site, and we talked for a while as the finishing touches were made on the barbecue, the chicken, the burgers, brats, hot dogs, etc. what a memorable feast.

Before we began the great feast, cousin Antoine led us in prayer and thanksgiving. Then it was on, and on, and on. I had seconds and thirds. I know I will fast and detox when I get back home, but not today. I felt so good; we as a family felt so good. This would not be a day of inaction—no, sir.

We had our version of the "Hunger Games" in the picnic. What I mean is, after we finished eating, there would be a competition where those of us who chose to participate would do various semi-athletic, unscripted activities. We would be in two-man teams. My sister Dee and I were together, Dana and Teddy were together, Wanda and another cousin were together, Kristin and her brother John were together, and Brianna and her husband Mike were together—with Landon Xavier in utero. There were other cousins paired together. I believe we had about twelve teams of two doing various relays and games of skill for six different events. One was transporting a cotton ball with a plastic spoon while moving at top speed—if the cotton ball fell, you had to start over. We also had to transport water from one bucket to another bucket, as quickly as possible using only two sponges. Another event was where one tried to toss a Frisbee through a hula hoop over your partners head at a distance greater than thirty feet. One other event was using a bolo lasso to hit various rungs of different heights for different points. Another was a water balloon toss without "breaking" the balloon. One more activity was a combination of bocce ball and billiards played on sand (don't ask). The final activity was to find a small piece of cookie under a plate full of whipped cream using only your mouth.

The games were enjoyable and interesting. Other than the water balloon toss, I had not played any of these games before, and it was truly a challenge. My sister has always been athletic, so I had a great partner. After the point totals came out, Dee and I as well as Brianna and Mike tied for second place. A couple of my cousins from Jimmie's side of the family won. What a day this was.

After more food and drink, we decided to burn off some more calories playing volleyball. What a game—I mean, we had several games. When it lightly rained, the ladies left the volleyball court, but as the rain intensified, we would all end up under the roof-like structure over our numerous picnic tables and food. I did not mind. This gave me more time to talk to cousins I had not had a chance to earlier. Cousin Jimmie also had a deck of cards, and he was introducing family members to a new card game. I took this opportunity to continue to mingle. Slowly but surely, relatives began to leave as the rain began to subside. We probably won't see each other again until two more years in 2016 in Chicago (my cousin Wanda volunteered). I had to take this opportunity to say goodbye, just in case some relatives would not make it to church tomorrow or the following brunch at the banquet hall.

As the relatives slowly cleared out, my siblings, niece, nephew, cousins, and I, as well as Jimmie's family, began to clean up and prepare to leave. What a phenomenal day. I did not want it to end. Jimmie and his family left. Wanda, Kristen, and John would check out the sites in Charlotte. My cousin Debbie would do some reading, and my siblings, niece, nephew, daughter, and son-in-law agreed to meet back at the hotel for a get-together one last time before tomorrow's finale.

After purchasing some beverages and snacks, we met back at the hotel in my sisters' room. There, my siblings and Teddy played cards while I was busy going over family history and explaining people's pictures to my daughter, son-in-law, and niece. You really don't know how much you know until you have to explain it to someone else. I felt like a griot of West Africa, who were the human archives of a tribe, going back generations and generations on memory alone. They recounted not only families and their origins but also historic events surrounding each generation. I even surprised myself with what I was able to recall. Since all my living siblings are older than me (Teddy's dad has been deceased for twelve years), if there was a relative or event I was stuck on, they were there to verify a photo, an individual, or a story.

This is what life is about—family and passing information from one generation to the next. I am so blessed to be able to have this honor. I felt like an elder tribesman. And to think my grandson Landon was there in utero, and according to some West African beliefs, my ancestors were there as well. Maybe even the white ones.

Mike was just as interested in the stories as my daughter and niece. I thought it was a good thing since Mike is white and their child/my grandchild will share a number of cultures happily.

I kept talking and my siblings played cards late into the night. Brianna and Mike were getting tired. I don't blame them since they drove down yesterday and really haven't had a good night's rest since they were in Virginia a couple of days ago. The adrenaline was wearing off—I understood.

I accomplished my objective; if I should die, the information has been transferred from one generation to the next, not just to Brianna, Mike, and Landon but to my niece Alisha and my nephew Teddy as well. If I had to leave this realm (I hope I don't), I could leave in peace. Some people may think that's dramatic, but if you look at it from my facts—my father died at forty-seven, my mom at fifty-three, my brother at thirty, and I was now fifty-one—I don't take my mortality for granted. I take it very seriously. Life is gravy after this point. My most immediate goal is to see the beautiful face of my grandson, Landon Xavier. We all bade each other a good night and settled in for a restful night before church the next day.

Sunday was somber because we would be going our separate ways later. I was sad, but I put on a happy face, knowing we would at least be here until midafternoon. The church service was more subdued and reflective than the rousing, powerful sermon in Burlington a year ago. Both messages were poignant and valuable, just different styles of preaching—both effective. The family was introduced to the congregation (like last year), which is always very humbling and a great honor at the same time.

We definitely had a lot to be thankful for. Just the fact we could find each other (post-slavery) spread out at least among eight states across the US, especially considering the sketchy information kept about slaves and their lives, is a testament to family. A strange irony is that if we had not been directly related (genetically) to the plantation owner's family, I don't know if we would have gotten this far so easily. The white members' births and locations provided a timeline and a geographical area to focus on. The written documents gave an indication who was with who and the possibilities of various unions. Our family history continues to be an ongoing detective story; maybe one of you reading this will give me a clue one day.

After the inspiring church service was over, we would head over to the banquet hall for our last southern meal (for a while). It would be an excellent sit-down dinner where we were to be served by caterers, and we would have a multimedia presentation of our roots, given by my cousin Jimmy himself. He asked Wanda and myself to give a background of the lineage of Charles Henry Bethel, which we happily did. I even sited a passage in *Roots* (pages 830-832) by Alex Haley, which mentioned the wagon train from Alamance County to Lauderdale County in West Tennessee. The relatives clapped after our presentation.

I gave Cousin Jimmie a signed copy of Regina Carter's CD "Southern Comfort". The artist explores her roots on the CD musically. Her violin almost talks to the listener, telling of Regina's West African and Finnish ancestry, which she highlighted with her autograph. She was very pleased when I told her that I too would be going to a family reunion. She also got her information from Ancestry.com.

Cousin Antoine led us in prayer and told us to be mindful of those who had passed on and those who were presently ill. Cousin Jimmie and Angela presented awards for various activities through the weekend: Cousin Wanda for musical chairs, one cousin for winning the ice breaker bingo, my daughter Brianna for having the newest family member, and a couple of cousins for winning the "Hunger Games" competition we had at the picnic the day before.

There were a few other "gifts" given; it was done in good fun, very humorous. Cousin Hayward gave the genealogy of George Bethel, who was a brother to Oscar and Charles Henry but not the same father. Cousin Hayward gave us a sample of his humor; he is very upbeat. He is also a stand-up comedian who is booked with a cruise line in 2015.

It was now midafternoon, and I did not know how traffic would be. We would all be leaving on three separate flights, so I wanted to get to the airport as soon as possible. We hugged each other hard. We would definitely miss this newfound family of ours. In two years, the relatives will be coming to Chicago for the next reunion. Wanda took the initiative to volunteer Chicago and promised quite a party—and Cousin Wanda is quite the organizer. She also enjoys a good party. I cannot wait until 2016.

There was small talk at the airport, and we reminded each other how happy we were to see each other and how much we would miss each other. We talked of the highs of the last forty-eight hours. Mike and Brianna drove back to Virginia as we were leaving the banquet hall (not before receiving many hugs and well-wishes for the baby). We embraced as tightly and safely as possible with someone who was six months pregnant. I could not wait for the birth of my grandchild. The projected date was October 6. I had it circled on the calendar.

All my relatives made it safely home and without incident. Now it was time to buckle down to my old semi-veggie diet and supplements. I still had my oatmeal in the morning and green juice throughout the day. In a way, I was happy to get back to my old routine. There is only so much of that rich, wonderful, and delicious southern food that one can have before becoming addicted. I made it out just in time.

Chapter Thirteen

I was ready to be a grandpa. All he had to do now was show up. I was calling every week (which is a lot for me). September ended, and I wanted the baby to get here. Brianna was so fortunate that her mom could take off to be with her during the month of October. Her mother had been through this three times: first Brianna, then a year later came Brian, and two years after that, Brandon. Cynthia was definitely a person Brianna needed. Mike was also very helpful and attentive, more so than most new fathers. Both of them would be with Brianna in the delivery room. She had a winning team. It seemed Mike and Brianna had all the necessary items they needed at home, and Cynthia would coordinate and help out as needed for the month of October.

September was done. The days seemed like forty-eight instead of twenty-four hours. The projected date of October 6 came and went without Landon. This is not unusual for a first child. October 7 came and went. Then October 8 came and Landon went. I received a text at 8:51 EST: "At the hospital... 6 cm dilated." She was 1.5 centimeters the previous day.

At about 12:02 a.m. on October 9, 2014, I received the text: "just came out." He was here; Landon Xavier Scanlon has arrived. I was at work, and I could not wait for my break at 1:00 a.m. so I could get more details. I wanted to fly out at that moment, but there were no flights available at this time anyway. The earliest flight that I would be able to take was late that night, getting into Norfolk, Virginia, early Friday morning, and visitation was from 8:00 a.m. to 8:00 p.m. My flight was late due to the result of some sabotage that took place at an Aurora, Illinois, facility that affected both O'Hare and Midway flights.

By the time I got in, got my rental car, and got to the hotel, it was around 2:00 a.m. I felt like I couldn't sleep, although I felt like I had been up since I received the news the previous day. Morning came quickly. I showered, ate, and prayed, and it was off to Portsmouth Naval Hospital. I stayed at a nearby hotel, so I was there in a matter of minutes. My heart was racing. My daughter had given me the room number earlier. Brianna was easy to find. I knocked on the door and slowly opened it. The curtains were drawn. I asked if I could enter. She responded, "Sure, Dad." She was feeding/nursing Landon.

Landon Xavier—I could see him now in the flesh, the same little boy that kicked at my hand when I had placed it on my daughter's tummy at the family reunion a few months ago. He was so quiet and still in the comfort of his mother's bosom. It reminded me of when my daughter was in the comfort of her mother's bosom twenty-seven years ago. I congratulated Mike after I kissed Brianna. What a beautiful sight. At this point, there was no race, just family and a spectrum of shades from light to dark.

As soon as he was done nursing, my daughter let me hold him. I sat in a very comfortable rocker in the room. Everything seemed to fade as I looked into those intense eyes that seemed to absorb me. I felt the connection with him and throughout all the ages. I was thinking of all the people I thought he may look like. I gave up after a while just to enjoy the moment, this moment of being someone's grandfather. I could feel those seven pounds getting heavier but enjoying every bit of the load. I then thought of my daughter who carried this little person as they progressed in weight, and the changes her body had to go through to accommodate those changes.

The cycle was now complete. Whether I find the origins of my great-great-great-grandmother Nidra or not is not more important than what I have just found—peace. I am sure that as he grows, there may be issues of identity or not. The world is rapidly changing, and by the time Landon is twenty-eight, the demographics will change from light to dark in America. Landon will be a part of that future, that change. How ironic to be in Virginia holding this beautifully mixed child. It was in Virginia where the Loving couple's case went all the way to the Supreme Court overturning the previous laws prohibiting interracial marriage close to fifty years ago.

Here I am holding this beautiful child of the future—one between black and white. He will witness so many changes. He will be a part of so many changes. Hopefully, he will be a contributor to change what he can. What a tall order. For now, rest, and enjoy the comfort of your grandfather's arms, as he is enjoying you being there. For now, the search for Nidra can wait; our identity is what we make of it.

Thank you, Landon Xavier. You are a good teacher.

Between Black and White
(for Landon Xavier)

Born a little after midnight. After the night, beginning the day.
Your little life will show us the way. The sign of Libra, the balanced scales, may you always be patient and always be fair.
Listen twice as much as you speak. The Lord gave us two ears and one mouth for a reason.
Respect authority, yet challenge it if you must.
Progress cannot be made without a little push.
God has already given you the gifts you need in this life.
Your purpose is to open the packages, thanking him by the way you live your life.
May you achieve balance in both worlds without having to choose either one.
May your childhood innocence affect everyone.
In you we see that love is right.
In that space between black and white.

Tony Bethel
(Your Granddad)

I would like to end with two great quotes from two great men assassinated for their beliefs. The first is from John Lennon who shares the same birthday of my grandson—October 9th. The quote is:

"Give peace a chance"

The second quote is from a man who went through great racial turbulence in his life. He was black but also part white. The quote was taken from an interview with Pierre Berton on January 19, 1965 (roughly a month before Malcolm X's assassination). The man is Malcolm X, the quote may surprise you:

"I believe in recognizing every human being as a human being, neither white, black, brown, or red"

Made in the USA
Middletown, DE
11 June 2017